Public Planet Books

A series edited by Dilip Gaonkar, Jane Kramer,
Benjamin Lee, and Michael Warner

Public Planet Books is a series designed by writers in and
outside the academy—writers working on what could be
called narratives of public culture—to explore questions
that urgently concern us all. It is an attempt to open the
scholarly discourse on contemporary public culture, both
local and international, and to illuminate that discourse
with the kinds of narrative that will challenge sophisticated readers, make them think, and especially make
them question. It is, most importantly, an experiment in
strategies of discourse, combining reportage and critical
reflection on unfolding issues and events—one, we hope,
that will provide a running narrative of our societies at
this particular fin de siècle.

Public Planet Books is part of the Public Works publication project of the Center for Transcultural Studies,
which also includes the journal *Public Culture* and the
Public Worlds book series.

Don't

public planet books

Don't

A Reader's Guide to the Military's Anti-Gay Policy

Janet E. Halley

——————

DUKE UNIVERSITY PRESS   *Durham and London, 1999*

© 1999 Duke University Press
All rights reserved
Printed in the United States
of America
on acid-free paper ∞
Typeset by Tseng Information
Systems, Inc. in Bodini Book.
Library of Congress Cataloging-
in-Publication Data appear on
the last printed page of this book.
The text of this volume first
appeared, in different form, as
"The Status/Conduct Distinction
in the 1993 Revisions to Military Anti-Gay Policy: A Legal
Archaeology" in *GLQ* 3, nos.
2–3, 1996.

For Libby

The number of discharges for homosexual status—or conduct—sorry—is actually—appears to be going down[.]
—*Department of Defense Regular Briefing*
(May 10, 1993) (DOD1)

The regulations concerning homosexual conduct in the Navy, while lengthy and detailed, are actually quite straight forward [*sic*].
—*Memorandum of Department of the Navy Code 34 Re: Homosexual Administrative Discharge Board/Show Cause Hearings (June 1994) (Navy1)*

Contents

Acknowledgments

I had so much help writing this book that I feel lonely now that it's done. Steve James Jackson and Steven C. Gonzales did grippingly good research. Librarians Andy Eisenberg, Paul Lomio, Iris Wildman, Erika Wayne, and Andrew Gurthet assembled documents against all odds; librarians at military libraries around the country assisted Paul Lomio in extracting obscure historical records. Indeed, Paul Lomio, Erika Wayne, and Andrew Gurthet were so creative, energetic, and successful in finding rare documents that they invented a way to make them generally available: Stanford Law Library's website "Don't Ask, Don't Tell, Don't Pursue," http:// dont.stanford.edu (check it out!). Michelle M. Benecke, Greg Bonfiglio, David H. Braff, Suzanne Goldberg, Roy Hawkins, Jana Kramer, Herbert W. Mondros, Paul Schmittberger, Randall Tietjen, Evan Wolfson, Marc Wolinsky, and the National Lawyers Guild Military Law Task Force supplied crucial items. Over the course of this work I enjoyed the generous research support of the Dorothy Redwine Estate, of Richard W. Weiland, and of the

Robert E. Paradise Faculty Scholarship for Excellence in Research and Teaching.

I am also thankful to audiences and readers who helped me through an unusually long and arduous process of sorting out confusing, contradictory elements of the 1993 debates over military anti-gay policy. Indeed, with such abundant and intelligent help it is particularly important for me to emphasize that any and all errors of fact, interpretation, and judgment are mine. The book benefited from presentation to audiences at the New York University Humanities Council Faculty Research Colloquium, the "Publics and Privates" conference at Cornell University, Stanford University's Letter of the Law Seminar, and legal studies seminars at the University of Arizona School of Law, the University of Miami Law School, and Columbia University Law School. Many people read drafts with characteristic acuity and generosity: Guyora Binder, Judith Butler, Fernando Rodriguez Casas, Richard Ford, Robert Gordon, Jody Greene, Thomas Grey, David Halperin, Mark Kelman, Andrew Koppelman, William B. Rubenstein, Jonathan Simon, William H. Simon, and Michael Warner. As I struggled to make sense of military anti-gay policy I also relied on the advice, support, and relentless critical edge of Barbara A. Babcock, Paul Brest, Barbara H. Fried, Roberta L. Krueger, Michael Moon, Andy Parker, Nancy Sorkin Rabinowitz, Eve Kosofsky Sedgwick, Jan Schrieber, and Kendall Thomas.

And, of course, without Elizabeth Faye Potter nothing.

Introduction

The American public remembers the 1993 revisions to military anti-gay policy wrong. First, people think that the new policy is more lenient toward gay men and lesbians in uniform, less anti-gay, and less homophobic than the policy in place when President Clinton took office. Second, they think that Clinton should get the credit for this change. And, third, they think that the change achieved in 1993 marked the end of discharging servicemembers for their status and the beginning of discharging them for their conduct. The new policy is supposedly fairer because it sanctions servicemembers not for "who they are" but for "what they do."

Wrong, wrong, and wrong again. The new military policy is *much, much worse* than its predecessor. Clinton's Department of Justice is almost certainly to blame for this. The department was the source of the most alarming innovation in the new policy—a new set of rules that allows homosexual conduct to be inferred from supposed homosexual status. The only reforms Clinton proposed that would have moved away from status regulation toward conduct regulation were deleted from the statute finally adopted by Congress. Although Clinton's administration has had the leeway to reintroduce some of the reforms in Department of Defense regulations, it has consistently failed to do so.

Every moving part of the new policy is designed to *look like* conduct regulation in order to *hide* the fact that it turns decisively on status. At least the old policy was as bad as it looked; problems of deceptive appearance, ruse, tautology, and outright misrepresentation make the new policy a regulatory Trojan Horse.

The city that this Trojan Horse invades is nothing other than heterosexual identity. In the process of making the new policy more anti-gay, the drafters of the 1993 revisions also made it more arbitrary, wide-reaching, and unpredictable. Doing things that make your commander think you are gay—like making pro-gay statements, or cutting your hair a certain way, or not fitting the gender stereotype of the sex you belong to—can be the basis for an inference that you have engaged in or might someday engage in homosexual conduct; and once your commander draws that inference you can be discharged from the military unless you can prove that you have *no propensity* to engage in such conduct. Of course, most heterosexuals will be able to prove "no propensity," not by proving specific acts of erotic conduct but by bringing in evidence of their heterosexuality more generally—that is, of their status. That's not as easy as you might think, particularly when the ultimate goal is to prove a negative—and not just a negative about a state of fact, but a negative about something as amorphous and hard-to-pin-down as sexual identity. They can never be quite sure what the outcome would be. Indeed, since they can never be quite sure what their commander will think creates an inference that they are gay, they can never be entirely confident that they'll never fall into this danger. Servicemembers who "really are" heterosexual lost a great deal of security when the 1993 revisions were adopted.

Acting viciously anti-gay is probably the best way to avoid this danger. As Ted Allenby, a Marine dishonorably discharged for homosexuality during World War II, said in response to Studs Terkel's question "Did you take part in the banter?": "Of course. You have to, otherwise somebody'd suspect you. You develop quite a repertory of tricks to prevent detection. Be even more vociferous than everybody else" (Terkel 180). If that is how things work out in a particular unit—and advocates say there are plenty of units where this is precisely what is happening—the policy will be a one-way ratchet ever tightening the screw of homophobia.

As hard as the policy is on heterosexuals, it is proportionately harder on gay servicemembers. Indeed, it discriminates against them because of their status as gay men, lesbians, and bisexuals. It is written to provide a plausible, smooth-sounding constitutional justification— one that courts have, on the whole, swallowed whole—but it should be held unconstitutional nevertheless. Even if that never happens, it should be abandoned as bad policy.

The military anti-gay policy in place when Clinton was inaugurated was explicitly status-based. You could be discharged from service if you were found to *be homosexual,* and if you said you were gay you could stay in uniform only if officials found that you were "*not a homosexual or bisexual.*" The Clinton reforms were supposed to switch the focus of the policy, from status to conduct: "not what they are, but what they do" (Cong. 7 5–6). What actually emerged from the legislative process was a complex new set of regulations that discharge people on grounds that tie status to conduct and conduct to status in surprising, devious, ingenious, perverse, and frightening ways. Sure, servicemembers are required not to "tell," and officers are supposed not to "ask." But the most important innovation is a provision that all discharges for homosexuality will be grounded on the servicemember's commission of conduct that would manifest, to a reasonable person, a

4   propensity to engage in homosexual acts. "Telling" isn't speech in this formulation: it is an act that manifests a propensity. It could include getting caught *in flagrante delicto* with a person of the same sex, or caught holding hands affectionately with a person of the same sex — or doing anything that a "reasonable person" would think might indicate a capacity to enjoy same-sex sex. This is where the famous "rebuttable presumption" comes in: engaging in any such conduct sets up a presumption of a propensity *that the servicemember has to rebut.* That is, if you have been found to have engaged in conduct that manifests a propensity to engage in same-sex erotic or sexual acts, you are going to be discharged unless *you* can prove that you have *no such propensity.* Transcripts of boards convened to hear individual cases indicate what anyone would expect: that, based on evidence of conduct alone, you can't prove *no propensity.* Except in a few aberrational cases, you need to prove your status, and your status has got to be heterosexual.

And who is this reasonable person? The new regulations provide no check on a commander's decision about what a reasonable person would think manifests a propensity. When a commander thinks that befriending a "known homosexual" manifests a propensity, that's *de jure* reasonable. When a commander thinks that women who want to serve in the military are probably lesbians, every act of every woman in that unit manifests a propensity. These inferences, once drawn, will also quickly become *de facto* reasonable. It is an important part of the argument of this book that the "reasonable person" feature of the new policy may be its most dangerous element, not because it allows commanders to be arbitrary, but because their social semiotics of sexual orientation statuses are, under the policy, actually and really, reasonable. The "reasonable person" feature requires every servicemember to imagine a lexicon of conduct-that-my-commander-thinks-to-manifest-a-propensity, and to avoid using any terms from that word list (or perhaps I should say, gestures from that playbook). Far from setting up an objective yardstick that will allow servicemembers to "play by the rules," the "reasonable person" feature of the policy has made every unit with a commander intent on enforcing the policy into a paranoid semiotic system in which the signification of homosexuality and of heterosexuality are always changeable, always at stake, always electrically important.

The new regulations are based on a 1986 Supreme Court decision, *Bowers v. Hardwick*[1] and translate the rhetoric of that baneful decision into rules of conduct for everyday life in the military.

The *Hardwick* case arose from the arrest of Michael Hardwick on charges of consensual sodomy under Georgia's sodomy statute. The prosecutor eventually dropped the charges, but Hardwick worried that he could be forced to defend himself eventually. He had good reason for worrying. As Kendall Thomas reports, Hardwick had been persistently and perhaps obsessively harassed ever since a member of the Atlanta police force found out that he worked at a gay men's bar. This officer obtained a warrant to arrest Hardwick on a charge of drinking in public, walked into his home and then into his bedroom (purportedly to serve the warrant), and found him there engaged in fellatio with another man. Hardwick was then charged with sodomy. Prosecutors later dismissed the charge, a move that left it hanging like Damocles's sword over Hardwick's head, ready to drop at any moment that the Atlanta police convinced prosecutors that Hardwick's "homosexual conduct"—anything from publicly identifying as gay, to going to gay bars, to having sex in the privacy of his home with other, consenting men— became a public menace (Thomas, "Beyond the Privacy Principle" 1437–39).

Hardwick challenged the sodomy charge as a violation of privacy rights he enjoyed under the U.S. Constitution. The Supreme Court ruled against him, holding that the states (and implicitly the federal government) could criminalize sodomy if they wished. The Court's decision is notorious for its egregiously homophobic declarations. The majority opinion derided the arguments upon which Hardwick had prevailed in the Court of Appeals as "facetious," and the concurring opinion of Chief Justice Burger gratuitously cited Blackstone to describe same-sex sodomy as " 'the infamous *crime against nature*,' " "an offense of 'deeper malignity' than rape, a heinous act 'the

very mention of which is a disgrace to human nature'"
(*Hardwick* 194, 197 [quoting 4 W. Blackstone, *Commentaries* 215]).

Justice Powell, who cast the decisive fifth vote against Hardwick, later indicated that he had "probably made a mistake in that one" (Agneshwar). *Hardwick* should be a derelict upon the waters of the law, but the 1993 revisions to military anti-gay policy gave it alarming new life. They did so by exploiting a deep, complex ambiguity in the text of the *Hardwick* decision itself. *Hardwick*'s complexity arises because Georgia's sodomy statute prohibits same-sex *and* cross-sex sodomy: *no one* can engage in fellatio, cunnilingus, or anal intercourse in Georgia without committing a felony. This is a ban on certain acts; it makes no reference to the kind of person who might commit them. Hardwick's argument before the Supreme Court was that the entire statute was unconstitutional: his brief spoke not of the rights of particular kinds of persons, but of the limits that privacy rights put on the powers of the state. But the majority framed the case as a challenge to the application of the statute in this case, to Hardwick alone, and posed itself a question that put the relationship between sodomy-the-act and Hardwick-the-homosexual at the crux of its decision: "The issue is whether the Federal Constitution confers a fundamental right *upon homosexuals* to engage in *sodomy*. . . ." (*Hardwick* 190; emphasis added).

From the majority Justices' perspective, sodomy was a bad act, and homosexuals were a bad type of person. But each is bad for different—indeed, sometimes, for inconsistent—reasons. If sodomy is bad, for instance, then homosexuals and heterosexuals who do it are bad.

7

If homosexuals are bad, we are bad whether we've engaged in sodomy or not. To hold both of these positions with consistency, you have to be willing to say that many, many heterosexuals are bad. *This* the majority Justices never acknowledged: in their hands, sodomy and homosexual persons became metonyms of one another. They wanted the badness of each to contaminate the other — while heterosexual personhood remained out of the picture, protected from the taint with which it was logically involved. By linking conduct and status, the Court assured that it could vilify fellatio, cunnilingus, and anal intercourse, without feeling the pull to truth-telling that might have tugged at them had they faced up to the enthusiasm with which heterosexual couples throw themselves into these very acts.

The resulting confusion allowed some out-and-out legerdemain to escape detection. First, let me restore the elision I made just a moment ago: "The issue is whether the Federal Constitution confers a fundamental right upon homosexuals to engage in sodomy and hence invalidates the law of the many States that still make *such conduct* illegal and have done so for a very long time" (*Hardwick* 190; emphasis added). Strictly speaking, "such" of "such conduct" refers to sodomy only, but the sentence depends crucially on its personal reference. And so the Court went on to answer its question as though "such conduct" referred to sodomy-as-defined-by-the-homosexuals-whose-characteristic-act-it-is.

By leaving the act/identity ambiguity open, moreover, the Court remained always ready to focus on "act" or "status" according to the expediencies of the situation. The claim that "homosexual sodomy" has been transhistorically condemned, for example, was an important part of the Court's reason for saying that the Framers of the Bill of Rights and the Fourteenth Amendment would never have intended to protect it from criminalization. The problem with this claim is that sodomy has been defined so variously through history—in an early American case the term seems to have meant consensual sexual intercourse of an adult man with a girl—that it can't support any cogent inference of the Framers' intent. It is not for nothing that Foucault described sodomy as "that utterly confused category" (Foucault 101; see also Goldberg, *Reclaiming Sodom* and *Sodometries;* Halley, "Reasoning" 1751–67). The Court thus had to engage in some very sloppy, inaccurate, self-blinding history to make its historical point: it had to resort to the homosexual person as the device for unifying this wildly disparate history and for providing the basis for a claim that the Framers had a coherent intention about whether or not it was included within basic constitutional liberties. This piece of the Court's logic *appears* to depend on acts, but *actually* depends on persons.

Elsewhere its logic *appears* to depend on persons, but actually plays fast and loose with acts. I am pointing to an out-and-out logical contradiction in the Court's rejection of Hardwick's argument that the sodomy statute lacked a rational basis. The statute, intoned the majority, rationally expressed a popular judgment that homosexuality was morally wrong. Of course, the statute could do no such thing, unless it also expressed a popular judgment that heterosexuality was morally wrong. But there is expedience even here: by collapsing the quite different ideas of "sodomy" and "homosexual," and affirming the wrongness of both, the Court manages to confer invisibility not only on heterosexual sodomy, but on heterosexual status *tout court.*

Heterosexual acts are, after all, just as felonious under Georgia's statute as homosexual ones. The same was true at the time under the laws of Washington, D.C., Virginia, and Maryland—probably an exhaustive list of the places where the majority Justices normally spent their most intimate hours. By reasoning that the Georgia statute rationally expresses disapproval of homosexual persons, the Justices masked their own status as potential sodomites *even if* they never strayed from the class of heterosexuals.

This is both the Justices' bid for immunity, and their offer of immunity to anyone willing to identify as heterosexual. It is hedged round with risk: immunity can be granted to heterosexuals only inasmuch as danger is the lot of homosexuals; and it can be a meaningful bribe only as long as it is uncertain. The modus operandi of this nasty little bit of superordination is to work the ambiguous relationship between sodomy (the act) and homosexual personhood (the status) for all the safety and danger it can generate. The new military anti-gay policy is, in this respect, *Hardwick* writ large.

Discourses are semi-rigid, semi-fluid systems of language, definition, and gesture that assign and organize meaning, often by contradiction and tension. They encompass us and limit our possibilities, so they are rigid; we actually do make changes in them, small and large, sometimes intentionally, so they are semi-rigid. They are full of puns, mistaken identities, and concepts passing under the color of other concepts—that is to say, they are permeated by language—and so they are fluid. But there are times when we can observe these slippages, and decide whether we will go along with them, so they are semi-fluid.

All of these features of discourse are present in the handling of act and status in *Hardwick*. The Court both inherited and gave new shape to the problematic relationship between sexual acts that everybody does and homosexual identity. It exploited the ability of acts to pass for status, and vice versa, and yet exposed itself to criticism for doing so. The fact that there are contradictions and tensions in the *Hardwick*'s discourse of act and status hardly weakens its power as a shaper of discourses. The condemnation of sodomy needs the concept of homosexual persons to limit its reach; but the condemnation of homosexual persons needs the concept of sodomy to find a link back to eras when sexual abomination was defined without reference to persons. To be sure, this is contradictory, and it's normal to say that is a weakness. But the smooth way in which each side of the contradiction cures the logical ills of the other links them together with amazing tightness, while giving them an almost shimmering liquidity. Noticing that strict logical thinking would undo some of these links is useful, but not enough to make apparent the full complexity, and the possibility for political manipulation, that the discourse of act and status obtained in *Hardwick*.

Legal discourses don't operate in this abstract way alone, moreover. It is an important theme of this book that the discourse of act and identity unfolds in the legal system because of steps taken by particular institutional players. To understand legal discourses, you have to pay attention to the peculiarities of particular institutional settings. In the case of military anti-gay policy, that means attending to all the technological specificities of the long, complex driveshaft that connects the act/status distinction to the material project of discharging a particular person from the military service. The question "What is the discourse of acts and statuses?" needs to be rephrased: "How did the specific historical and institutional capacities of the legal system serve to connect *Hardwick's* discourse of acts and statuses to the drafting table on which the new military policy was written? How did the policy then shape the military hearing-boards' practices, and the culture of sexuality in military units?"

12

A remarkable range of institutional players contributed to the translation of *Hardwick* into a mode of military life. Though courts have been only part of this institutional technology, they not only provided *Hardwick* itself but also, in decisions extending its doctrinal reach, set up the status/conduct language in which the 1993 revisions speak.

Hardwick was a privacy case, not a discrimination case. Michael Hardwick claimed that the Constitution simply forbade the states from cutting into his liberty to decide what kinds of consensual, noncommercial sex to enjoy in his bedroom. He was not making the related discrimination claim, which would have conceded that the state can arrest people for consensual, noncommercial sex acts committed in their bedrooms in order to highlight the claim that it cannot do so unequally.

There are several good reasons to suppose that *Hardwick* tells us nothing about this antidiscrimination claim, much less antidiscrimination claims affecting child custody, employment rights, health benefits, access to public accommodations like housing, and so on. First, privacy law is distinct from equal-protection law. Except for the part of *Hardwick* that held that the Georgia statute rationally expressed Georgia voters' moral disapproval of homosexuality, none of the analysis in *Hardwick* has any counterpart in equal-protection analysis (and, as I have indicated, that part of *Hardwick* was itself deeply irrational). Second, most gay antidiscrimination claims don't involve sodomy at all: the gay plaintiff may never have engaged in anal intercourse, cunnilingus, or fellatio with anyone, much less with another person of his or her own sex; and the feature in the plaintiff that the defendant discriminated against is almost always an act of coming out, or an act of gender nonconformity, not a sex act. Antidiscrimination claims are almost always about public, even civic, relations: what has sodomy got to do with them?

Federal courts very soon began to provide an answer that made *Hardwick* binding law in equal-protection cases. Rejecting gay plaintiffs' claims that the Constitution allows extra scrutiny of anti-gay discrimination because sexual orientation is a "suspect class" (that is, a suspicious classification, presumed to be an improper one, for the decision maker to consider), courts held that *Hardwick* "forecloses [plaintiffs'] efforts to gain suspect class status for practicing homosexuals" because, "[i]f the [Supreme] Court was unwilling to object to state laws that criminalize *the behavior that defines the class*, it is hardly open to a lower court to conclude that state sponsored discrimination against the class is invidious" (*Padula* 103, emphasis added).

This holding, and several others like it, set up a di-

13

chotomy: gay plaintiffs would almost certainly lose when courts concluded that discrimination against them was based on disapproval of their sodomitical conduct, and they might well win when courts concluded that discrimination was based "merely" on their status.[2] This line of judicial opinions set up the basic dichotomy in which Clinton would claim that his new policy discharges people from the military not for what they are but for what they do. What he never seems to have understood is that the mutual contradictions and interdependence that tied status to conduct in *Hardwick* permeate the new military anti-gay policy.

This book is an archaeology of the 1993 revisions to military anti-gay policy. I examine the history of the 1993 revisions and their enforcement history, controversy by controversy, line by line, and at times even word by word. In the process of doing this analysis, I imagined that the 1993 revisions were an ancient text which modern readers inherited in a series of different versions, some clearly earlier than others. What was the idea behind each change? I asked myself.

Gradually a pattern emerged. The revisions were a gigantic multiplayer effort to generate and harness new meanings attributable to the status/conduct distinction. The changes themselves could be understood only if one knew who put them in, when, and in opposition to whom over what. I could have interviewed people directly to get this information, but—given the problem of false appearances, rhetorical gaming, and simple confusion that attended so much of the process—the answers I would have gotten would have required another set of interviews to explain them, and so on ad infinitum.[3] I decided to limit myself to the public record, and to draw conclusions about who did what, with what goals and to what effect, on the basis of the various policies under contention read synoptically, or side by side. The result is a voluminous bibliography, which appears at the end of this book. I have tried to keep references to it as simple as possible.

There are three chapters in this volume. Chapter 1 reviews the dizzying controversy that erupted just as Clinton took office, identifying key players, describing the kinds of negotiations they engaged in, and locating the draft revisions they proposed in their political contexts.

Chapter 2 reviews several struggles between Clinton and Congress (the latter not-quite-covertly backed up by the Joint Chiefs), in which Clinton actually did strive for a shift from status to conduct, and in which Congress refused him every time. Clinton wanted to say that homosexuals have served, and can serve, with honor; he wanted to enforce the military sodomy statute "evenhandedly"—that is, without regard to the sexual orientation of the accused or the sex of his or her partner; he wanted to eliminate a rule allowing people who had engaged in same-sex sex to stay in uniform if they could prove they were straight; and he wanted "don't tell" to be a narrow prohibition, balanced by a strict "don't ask" rule. Congress turned every one of these struggles into an across-the-board victory for status-based regulation.

Chapter 3 reviews the most important features of the military's new policy: the propensity clauses. Discharging servicemembers on grounds that they have manifested a propensity to engage in same-sex sex is *supposed* to anchor the claim that the new policy regulates conduct-not-status. A review of the origins of the propensity clauses, and the accompanying rebuttable presumption, as well as the early history of enforcement of the new policy, demonstrates that this supposition is mistaken. In the world of military anti-gay policy, "propensity" is an ambiguous term, referring just as much to homosexual status as to homosexual acts. Indeed, my research indicates that enforcers of the policy are fully aware of this ambiguity, and are perfectly willing to mislead courts about which meaning they are using. The resulting volatility recapitulates the act/identity dynamics of the *Hardwick* decision,

pushing them deep into the social world of the military. Heterosexual danger and immunity are, ultimately, the engine that makes the new policy self-enforcing in minute, terroristic ways, which will cause far more human suffering even than the occasional high-profile uses of the policy to discharge servicemembers for engaging in conduct that manifests a propensity.

The conclusion takes up the question "What should gay-friendly constituencies do about this depraved new regulation of sexuality?" I review—and criticize—the pro-gay litigation strategy that attacks military anti-gay policy as a regulation of status-not-conduct, and point instead toward constitutional arguments that are available to anyone who wishes to describe the policy accurately. These arguments are weighty: a judge who understands both the policy and equal-protection doctrine could easily hold the policy unconstitutional and put it out of our misery. But constitutional doctrine on irrational legislation is not well fitted to notice the really zany thing about the new military anti-gay policy. It is persistently discriminatory, but (unlike Jim Crow or the Gilded Cage) the worst features of the military anti-gay policy ensure that *no one benefits* because *no one belongs* in any extrinsic way to an advantaged or disadvantaged group; heterosexuality prevails, at the expense of both "homosexuals" and "heterosexuals." The ultimate question posed by the 1993 revisions to the military anti-gay policy, then, is this: How long will we use the coercive powers of the state to define, construct, and populate heterosexuality as a morally endorsable human and social class of persons?

17

1 The Negotiations and the Players

The story I'll tell involves the following cast of characters: President Clinton and his White House staff, Secretary of Defense Les Aspin, Attorney General Janet Reno (and the career Department of Justice lawyers working for her), the Joint Chiefs of Staff (including Colin Powell), the Joint Chiefs' subordinates at the Pentagon, and congressional leaders (including the Senate Armed Forces Committee chair Sam Nunn).

During Clinton's first year in the White House, these players struggled over five versions of military anti-gay policy. (1) Clinton inherited a set of Department of Defense regulations from the Reagan administration. (2) He then installed an "interim policy" suspending some of those regulations pending his announced effort to generate a new policy. (3) At Clinton's behest, Secretary of Defense Aspin drafted an executive order constituting new executive policy. (4) Congress ultimately spurned Aspin's proposal and adopted the first statute governing sexual orientation in the military. (5) And the Department of Defense proceeded to implement the statute by promulgating a series of new regulations. I will call these legal directives, respectively, (1) the Old DOD Policy, (2) the Interim Policy, (3) the New DOD Policy, (4) the Statute, and (5) the Implementing Regulations.[1]

By adopting the Statute, Congress seized control of military policy on sexual orientation from the executive branch. Executive control over these matters dates to 1962, when the Department of Defense produced the Old DOD Policy in order to impose a uniform regulation on all branches of service. As Clinton prepared to take office, many pro-gay constituencies naively assumed executive control to be permanent. Recalling President Truman's famous executive order banning racial segregation in the armed forces, they urged the new president to exercise his unilateral powers as commander in chief to rewrite military policy "with the stroke of a pen" (Healy, "Clinton Aides Urge"; Collins). And Clinton encouraged their hopes: in late 1992 President-elect Clinton indicated to the press that he intended to "lift the ban" on gays in the military, permitting homosexuals to serve and regulating only their conduct. Clinton seems to have realized only gradually that he did not, in fact, have unilateral powers in this area.

As much as pro-gay voices deprecated Clinton's retreat from unilateral executive action, he had no choice. Members of Congress and the Joint Chiefs promptly asserted their role and their power to block any revisions (Schmalz, "Difficult First Step"; Morganthau). Before Clinton had been in office one week, the Joint Chiefs had threatened to resign in protest against any new leniency toward gay men and lesbians in the armed services (Morganthau). In their initial meeting with Secretary of Defense Les Aspin, and to a lesser extent in their first meeting with President

Clinton, the Joint Chiefs objected to Clinton's proposed changes so vehemently and at such length that the press understood them to have issued a veto (Barr, "Hill Backs Gay Ban"; Schmitt, "Joints [*sic*] Chiefs"). At the same time members of Congress were warning that they would propose a bill codifying current anti-gay policy (Clymer; Schmitt, "Pentagon Chief"; "Gays in the Military"). Five days after the inauguration, the Senate's Democratic Majority Leader George J. Mitchell reported to the Clinton administration that its senatorial opposition had seventy votes. While the Joint Chiefs were engaging in political action verging on insubordination, Congress really does have power under Article I of the Constitution to legislate about the personal qualifications of servicemembers, and an executive order trenching on Congress's Article I powers cannot displace legislation. Clinton was the boss of the Joint Chiefs and could have compelled them to implement any executive order he issued, but he could not face off the coordinated opposition of photogenic military leaders and large congressional majorities.

Clinton then sought to draw key congressional and military figures into a negotiating process intended to tie them to its ultimate outcome. On January 29, 1993, he directed Secretary of Defense Aspin to draw up a "draft executive order" revising the Old DOD Policy and to submit it for presidential review by July 15 (WHI 112). He described the expected executive order itself as a "compromise" that "is not everything I would have hoped for or everything that I have stood for, but it is plainly a substantial step in the right direction" (WHI 109). And he lectured the press on the need for a compromise under the circumstances, reminding them "that any President's

Executive order can be overturned by an act of Congress" and noting that "Normally, in the history of civil rights advancements, Presidents have not necessarily been in the forefront in the beginning" (WHI 110). Aspin became Clinton's broker, charged to cement a deal between the White House, the Joint Chiefs, and Clinton's congressional opposition.

Aspin's shuttle diplomacy was officially due to end with the presentation of a proposed executive order on July 15. He was four days late. Between January 29 and July 19 the dramatis personae and their mode of operation in the conflict changed in several important ways.

Congress has been a persistent though not always effective advocate of its own role in military affairs: recall the War Powers Act. In this case, however, it had the power to legislate and used it to redesign Clinton's proposed process. Early in February, Senate Minority Leader Robert Dole proposed a bill requiring the president to submit any changes to existing executive policy on gays in the military as a bill (Cong.1 1263, Amendment No. 17). Congress adopted instead Democratic Senate Majority Leader George Mitchell's plan requiring that the Secretary of Defense review existing policy on the matter and submit any recommended changes to the president *and Congress* by July 15, 1993; and that the Senate Armed Services Committee hold hearings not only during the period of the Defense Secretary's review, but also after his report, to examine any changes he might recommend. Clinton signed this legislation as part of the Family and Medical Leave Act, his administration's first major piece of legislation. It effectively trumped his January 19 executive order to Aspin, and put two bits in Aspin's mouth.

The Mitchell bill situated Congress as a possible but not necessary final decision maker: legislation became a threat to be bargained away. Aspin issued the New DOD Policy on July 19 in the shadow of this threat. What Congress ultimately did, however, was to extract concessions by threatening legislation and then to legislate anyway. In November, it adopted the Statute as part of its 1994 military budget. The mere existence of a statute regulating military policy on sexual orientation is the mark of Clinton's institutional failure in the 1993 debates. Legislation in this area guarantees that Congress will continue to monitor executive branch policy: as Senator Strom Thurmond indicated, one purpose of the codification was to ensure that "Some future president won't be tempted to lift the ban" (Lochead). Not only that, Congress rejected several reforms that Clinton had paid dearly to achieve. The Statute is decisively more anti-gay than the New DOD Policy.

Understanding this outcome requires an assessment of the roles not only of the most visible public officials who produced it, but also of the less detectable players. Least detectable of all were pro-gay constituencies. Initially entranced by the "stroke of a pen" fantasy, they only slowly formed an organization dedicated to the upcoming struggle (Schmalz, "Gay Groups"; Burr). Even when formed, however, the Campaign for Military Service did not enjoy the uniform support of left and radical elements in gay and lesbian politics. Good reporting by Chandler Burr indicates that in mid-July, just when the most important, final changes were being made in the New DOD Policy, the White House cut off communications with the Campaign for Military Service while maintaining its conversations with military leaders and outspokenly anti-gay members of Congress (Burr).

Inaudibility at the top was echoed by silence at the grass roots: gay and gay-friendly servicemembers were locked out of the political process by the very policy they would have challenged. Clinton's Interim Policy introduced "don't ask" protections for gay *applicants* for military service, but none for gay and gay-friendly servicemembers. It provided that servicemembers who said they were gay would be placed in the "Standby Reserve" pending adoption of a new policy. Servicemembers seem to have known—though it is not clear how—that they had a choice: to stay outside the reach of the Interim Policy by remaining utterly silent in the public debate about their future, or to come out possibly at the expense of their careers. Marine Corps Sergeant Justin C. Elzie, Navy Lieutenant Richard Dirk Selland, and a very few others came out in the week after Clinton's inauguration, expressing confidence that he would keep his early promises (*Selland I* 14; *Elzie* 441). An unnamed intelligence officer tried to cut a third path by making "what he thought were anonymous public statements about what it is like to be gay in the military" and was processed under the Interim Policy when military officials managed to trace the statements back to him anyway. And several servicemembers came out in the express attitude of civil disobedience (Murdoch; Howlett). All were processed for discharge as soon as the Statute went into effect. Most gay servicemembers endured the 1993 debates in their closets, while congressional hearings amplified the prodigious din of their anti-gay fellows.

For military top brass, on the other hand, secrecy and obscurity were the techniques not of powerlessness but of strength. In late January the press criticized the Joint Chiefs for their obstreperous tone and recalcitrant posture at their first meetings with Aspin and Clinton: there was something unpatriotic, un-American, and unfriendly to established order in their failure to defer to the new president's authority as Commander in Chief (Schmitt, "Joints [*sic*] Chiefs"; Barr, "Who's in Charge"). Once the Joint Chiefs had secured a seat at the bargaining table, they no longer needed to take that kind of flak. They withdrew to become invisible but crucial players in the political process.[2] Aside from cameo appearances at committee hearings in which they stated their full agreement with executive policy initiatives, they devoted their attention to the back channel. What they did there escaped public scrutiny. The Joint Chiefs' success in keeping their vigorous participation in the political process secret allowed them to maintain a calm, statesmanlike demeanor and a tone of conciliation in public while insisting behind closed doors on steeply increased rigor in military antigay policy and procedure.

A similar obscurity covers the tracks of government lawyers, particularly Department of Justice attorneys who had gained expertise in defending the Old DOD Policy from constitutional challenge, DOD lawyers, and lawyers in the various military branches' Judge Advocate General (JAG) Corps. The following close reading of the 1993 revisions detects several points at which they must have played a key role, but because I have purposely limited myself to the examination of public documents, my conclusions are necessarily somewhat conjectural. If I am right, these institutional lawyers played a key role in designing the 1993 revisions' most dangerous elements, the propensity clauses. Here the full dynamism of the status/conduct distinction as it was used in *Hardwick* was translated into the form of living regulations.

2 Clinton Is to Conduct as Congress Is to Status

The Old DOD Policy was explicitly status-based. The explicit terms of these regulations authorized military officials to determine not only what servicemembers did but what they desired and intended, all with the aim of determining who they were. It required the separation of any servicemember deemed to be "homosexual" and defined the excludable servicemember as "a person, regardless of sex, who engages in, desires to engage in, or intends to engage in homosexual acts." If a servicemember merely stated that he or she was gay, the policy provided that he or she could remain in uniform only if "there is a further finding that the member is not *a homosexual or bisexual*" (emphasis added).

The Clinton administration proposed to change all that. When Secretary of Defense Les Aspin presented the New DOD Policy to the House Armed Services Committee, for instance, he explained that the purpose of revising the Old DOD Policy was to shift regulatory attention from status to conduct: "That is," as he said, "not what they are, but what they do" (Cong.7). The distinction began to sound like a mantra: Aspin insisted to the Senate Armed

Services Committee that, "[u]nder the new policy, *homosexual conduct* will continue to be grounds for discharge from military service. On the other hand, *sexual orientation* is considered a personal and private matter." Just in case that wasn't clear, Aspin went on to specify that "[u]nder the new policy *sexual orientation* alone will not bar individuals from military service unless it involves *homosexual conduct*" (Cong.7, emphases added). Meanwhile, Clinton told his military audience at Fort McNair that "the emphasis should be always on people's *conduct*, not their *status*"; "For people who are willing to play by the rules, . . . I believe . . . we should give them the chance to do so"; "there is no study showing [homosexuals] to be less capable or more prone to misconduct than heterosexual soldiers"; "misconduct is already covered by the laws and rules"; "[the first] essential element [of the new policy is that] . . . service men and women will be judged based on their *conduct*, not their *sexual orientation*" (WH4; emphasis added).

After Congress passed the Statute, Clinton, the White House, Aspin, and military leaders claimed that the Statute merely restated and codified the New DOD Policy (DOD6; DOD8; "Military Budget Is Passed")—a claim that has fooled one court into holding that *Congress's* effort to shift *from status to conduct* protects the Statute from constitutional challenge (*Able D* 1299). If Aspin's proposal regulates conduct not status, and the Statute merely codifies it, we'd be forced to conclude that the Statute regulates conduct, not status. Neither claim is true, however: together they hide both Aspin's and Congress's efforts to regulate status under the sign of conduct.

First claim first. The New DOD Policy and the Statute agree that people who engage in "homosexual conduct" should be excluded from military service and that homosexual orientation alone is not a basis for exclusion. Homosexual orientation alone is *unmanifested* homosexual orientation: the 1993 revisions hold out to gay men, lesbians, and bisexuals in uniform the promise of a safe haven for sexual orientation provided it be kept "personal and private" (Cong. 7). This formulation invokes the classic liberal rejection of state involvement in the management of statuses, but with a twist.

Statuses are legally determined, enduring personal relationships to society and the state: examples of statuses include serf, prince, felon, husband, wife. Statuses are (I would say by definition) determined in the public sphere, largely by law, and when not by law then by the very relationships among persons that they mediate and authenticate. Though statuses are often assumed to have deep subjective implications (it would be a deviant king who did not feel like a king; a deviant wife who did not feel like a wife), their *sine qua non* is legal or public ascription. Recent gay-rights struggles involve status in this more correct understanding only tangentially, for instance when they seek to obtain the benefits (and thus are willing to assume the status) of marriage, or when they seek to avoid the status of felon by decriminalizing same-sex sodomy. Gay-rights struggles simply don't have much quarrel with the fundamental liberal norm that it is a good thing for the state to leave statuses to private ordering, where the free choices of individuals can construct or dissolve them. Thus gay-rights advocates were disarmed, even co-opted, when advocates of the 1993 revisions promoted them on grounds that they took government out of the business of regulating status.

The hidden barb in apologetics for the 1993 revisions is the assumption that homosexuality, *as a status*, pre-exists legal ascription and will remain metaphysically the same whether the law recognizes it or not. This claim—that the law does not make homosexuals and in fact can entirely ignore them—rests on an implicit reification of sexual orientation as a form of personhood. Homosexual orientation is represented as status in the sense that it is **30** a type of personal character that inheres so deeply within a person that it constitutes a pervasive personal essence. Sexual-orientation status on this model is both real and intrinsic to individuals: it is not the nominal product of its apperception or a product of interaction among individuals. Sexual orientation as status is constituted in and as a secret inner core of personhood; thus it is not constituted in relationship, interaction, or representation. And so it has *nothing to do* with conduct.

In the metaphysics underlying conduct not status claims, then, conduct and status are not just conceptually distinct; they are real things that do not overlap in the real world. Conduct is, at least in a military context, always public while status is an inner and hence potentially secret characteristic of persons. Having divorced conduct and status in this way, Aspin proposed to set up separate regulatory frameworks for them: lots of regulation for the former, none for the latter.

But the 1993 revisions, even if they do not target people on the basis of their status, are nevertheless deeply, pervasively, and creatively ascriptive. Consider, for instance, the way in which the 1993 revisions respond to the most frequently expressed rationale for military anti-gay policy: the need for unit cohesion. This rationale assumes that bonding occurs only between people who are alike: difference is divisive. (That assumption doesn't always hold: the very same constituencies that introduce it to support military anti-gay policy also assert that heterosexual marriage achieves unit cohesion only because of difference.) It is possible to state the underlying problem addressed by the unit cohesion rationale as sexual conduct: some servicemembers won't trust their fellows if they are afraid that, having accepted psychological and physical intimacy, they will be unable to refuse sexual intimacy as well. This can't, of course, be a concern about rape or sexual harassment, both of which are already prohibited and are tolerated or punished depending on factors quite independent of the gravity of the sexual violations involved: the conduct that is the object of regulation here must be seduction.

But if that is true, the unit cohesion rationale conceals a basis in status, not conduct, regulation. This fact is hard to detect for two simple reasons. First, the policy's rationale turns not on the status of gay servicemembers but on the status of their straight companions. Second, the status actually at issue is not the status described by defenders of the 1993 revisions. They disavowed any effort to regulate status as an intrinsic, prelegal personality structure while writing new rules enabling the state to regulate status as the public construction and maintenance of what would otherwise be a quite fragile personal type. And to the extent that the 1993 revisions allow individuals with homosexual "status" to stay in the military as long as they don't "tell," the possibilities for seduction are increased rather than decreased: the very same provisions intended to provide protection for heterosexual personhood also exacerbate the anxiety that gives rise to the call for protection.

Finally, by covertly reverting to the constructivist meaning of "status," the unit cohesion rationale threatens its own premise that bonding requires sameness. Unit cohesion advocates see sexual orientation but not race as a "difference": in doing so they concede that difference is the effect rather than the cause of military personnel policy. Inasmuch as the features that make people different are themselves the cultural products of legal rules, difference and sameness are the results, not the premises, of legal policy.

The unit cohesion rationale thus mirrors the status/conduct dynamics of the *Hardwick* decision: (1) conduct and status are interdependent elements in the justification of military anti-gay policy; (2) we need to pierce the ambiguities of the term "status" (in *Hardwick*, of "conduct") in order to notice how it really functions in relation to "conduct" (in *Hardwick*, to "status"); (3) the interaction between status and conduct puts heterosexual, not homosexual, "status" at the crux of anti-gay policy; and (4) the case and the policy function not to address but to produce their justifications, particularly the justification of anxious heterosexual personhood.

Second claim second: the assertion that the 1993 revisions regulate conduct is most plausible when invoked to defend the Clinton administration's proposed policy; it entirely misrepresents the Statute. The Clinton administration did introduce several elements of more or less simple conduct regulation, but Congress in adopting the Statute eliminated every single one of them in favor of heavily status-inflected revisions. Each time it did so it moved further toward the regulation of persons.

Service with Honor or Absolute Incompatibility?

The Old DOD Policy had stated as its major premise that "Homosexuality is incompatible with military service." Press reports indicated that the White House pressed hard, against fierce resistance from the Joint Chiefs, to eliminate this stigmatizing language in favor of a statement that, while homosexual *conduct* was harmful, *homosexuals* could serve effectively and honorably (Schmitt, "White House"; Friedman, "Legal Concerns"). The struggles over the incompatibility statement capture the negotiations between the White House and the Joint Chiefs in a nutshell.

Clinton's preferred policy statement drew a status/conduct distinction and promised to regulate one and not the other. It is possible to say what the Joint Chiefs would have preferred instead, because their own immediate subordinates, convened as the Military Working Group (MWG), drafted a report for Aspin that stated an official uniformed response to Clinton's reform proposals. The MWG Report insisted that "*All homosexuality*" — "known" and "unknown," belonging to "practicing" and "nonpracticing homosexuals" — "*is incompatible with military service*" (DOD2 7; emphasis in original). A policy that puts this premise into effect would prohibit not only homosexual erotic conduct and professions of gay identity but even the most secret inner twinge of homoerotic feeling, and would justify vigorous and intimate detection efforts which the White House was determined to eradicate.

The Joint Chiefs never got what they wanted, but their two successive victories over the White House on the "incompatibility statement" indicate their deep hostility to Clinton's "status-not-conduct" goal. Aspin's New DOD Policy stated that "homosexuality is incompatible with military service": all that Aspin was able to preserve was the concession that this statement was only "a general rule" and the proviso that "Nevertheless the Department of Defense also recognizes that individuals with a homosexual orientation have served with distinction in the armed services of the United States." Later, the Statute appeared with a title — "Policy Concerning Homosexuality in the Armed Forces" — that reintroduced the Joint Chiefs' preferred term, and with no recognition that homosexuals could serve with distinction or even effectiveness. Instead, it expatiated exclusively, and at length, on the ways in which gay men and lesbians in uniform endanger national security. To be sure, the congressional findings persistently state these harms in terms of homosexual conduct and the dangers posed by servicemembers with a propensity to engage in it. But the gradual abrasion of the White House's preferred policy statement reflects the powerful intervention of drafting partners who resisted any implications of the status/conduct distinction that would impede military enforcement of a strong policy against *homosexuality.*

Direct Regulation of Sexual Contacts

One way of forcing a distinction between status and conduct — one that the pro-gay Campaign for Military Service
proposed in vain (Burr) — would have been to focus exclusively on sexual misconduct. The Uniform Code of Military Justice (UCMJ) prohibits rape, sodomy, sexual assault,
and attempts to commit any of those crimes. In addition
the military has used Article 133, prohibiting "conduct
unbecoming an officer and gentleman" and Article 134,
the "General Article," to regulate sexual behavior. None
of these provisions notices any difference between same-
sex and cross-sex conduct. If these provisions were enforced without regard to the sex of the people charged,
the military would indeed begin to punish violators "not
[for] what they are, but [for] what they do" (Cong. 7). Indeed, even if the definition of misconduct were limited
to same-sex erotic conduct more broadly construed, but
applied to *anyone* who indulged in it, without regard to
personal status, the revisions would have hewed to conduct rather than status.

Clinton sought both of these changes; Congress rejected them. The New DOD Policy proposed to prosecute
felony sodomy "in an even-handed manner," and to discharge servicemembers who engaged in same-sex conduct
without regard to their sexual orientations. Congressional
defeat of these provisions not only carved out privileges
for self-identified heterosexuals but also translated sexual
conduct into an index of status.

Sodomy. The most dramatic defeat of misconduct-based
regulation emerged in successive changes to the pro-

cedures governing sodomy prosecutions and separations from service on the grounds of homosexual conduct. The UCMJ prohibits all sodomy—no matter what the sex of the participants may be—as a felony subject to court-martial and criminal punishment. This is a facially neutral sodomy statute criminalizing cunnilingus, fellatio, and anal-genital contact even when these are performed by consenting persons of different genders. The military has been virtually the only U.S. jurisdiction willing to insist that such a statute criminalizes male-female fellatio that the complaining witness admits was consensual

(see *United States v. Fagg; United States v. Henderson*). But discriminatory enforcement of the UCMJ's sexual conduct provisions is the rule, not the exception: the military has sought and obtained a judicial holding that discriminatory enforcement of this statute against same-sex sodomy serves an important military purpose (*Hatheway* 1382), and has amassed a painful history of enforcing its sodomy statute primarily against same-sex conduct.

In a startling innovation, Aspin's New DOD Policy required commanders to "investigate allegations of violations of the Uniform Code of Military Justice in an even-handed manner without regard to whether the conduct alleged is heterosexual or homosexual." This abrupt break with military tradition, and with sexuality regulation in every state that maintains a sodomy statute, would have set up an expressly acts-based sodomy regime.

Implicitly refusing to regulate acts in any way that did not enforce status distinctions, however, Congress deleted this language from its Statute. And though the Department of Defense retained the "even-handed enforcement" provision in the Statute's Implementing Regulations (DODI2 D.3), it also introduced a new provision that produces a sharp return to status-based regulation of acts.

This procedural change, both elaborate in its institutional structure and hidden from view by burial in amendments to unpublished regulations, gives new meaning to Senator John Dingell's warning, "I'll let you write the substance . . . and you let me write the procedure, and I'll screw you every time" (Alexander 627). The amendment altered prior rules under which commanders had been required to refer all serious criminal charges, including sodomy charges, to military law enforcement agencies. Those agencies exercised primary jurisdiction over the ensuing investigations, charging decisions, and criminal proceedings.[1] The prior rules also gave commanders sole authority to initiate discharge proceedings arising from evidence of homosexual orientation short of criminal sodomy, assault, or solicitation. The Statute's Implementing Regulations alter this allocation of responsibility by providing that "Defense Criminal Investigative Organizations [DCIOs] and other DOD law enforcement organizations will normally refer allegations involving only adult consensual misconduct *to the servicemember's commander* for appropriate disposition" (DODI2 A; emphasis added). Sodomy and other felonious sexual conduct, if consensual, are no longer subject to criminal jurisdiction, but fall within the commander's power to impose less serious sanctions—including separation.

This apparently benign renunciation of criminal jurisdiction in fact generates a newly acute source of status differentiation. Referring all allegations of consensual sodomy from DCIOs to commanders produces starkly different procedural tracks for personnel accused of same-sex sodomy and those accused of cross-sex consensual sodomy. In a case involving female-male fellatio, for instance, a commander may, but need not, institute separation proceedings. But in cases involving male-male fellatio the commander's hands are tied: separation proceedings are mandatory.[2] Criminal sodomy allegations are, moreover, a particularly unfavorable place for discharge proceedings to begin: if found to be supported by credible evidence (there is no need for proof beyond a shadow of doubt), they may justify the imposition of an other-than-honorable discharge (Separation Regulations, **38** Part 2; Gilberd). Control of serious sexual misconduct has thus been shifted from a formally neutral procedure, to an explicitly discriminatory one.

To be sure, this element of the 1993 revisions removes criminal jurisdiction for all consensual sodomy. But the Implementing Regulations make it impossible to enforce the UCMJ sodomy ban in an "even-handed manner." Participants in cross-sex sodomy can hope for—and (let's be realistic) will often obtain—an indulgence that is legally withheld from participants in the same act committed with people of the same sex. Referring sodomy allegations to commanders will saddle some servicemembers with less-than-honorable discharges while reconfirming the military membership of others. "Status" in its 1993 sense, as the distinction between homosexual and heterosexual persons, is a necessary term of this phase of acts enforcement.

The *relationship* between conduct and status has also changed. The New DOD Policy's provision about sodomy enforcement defined conduct without reference to status. The procedural changes wrought by the Implementing

Regulations strip conduct of its definitional autonomy and resituate it in the dynamic relationship to status that it had in *Hardwick*. Fellatio is no longer oral-genital contact but *heterosexual* or *homosexual* conduct, the deed of a certain type of person. The distinct procedural scripts for conduct thus depend on status ascriptions.

The result is a set of distinctly asymmetrically fashioned statuses. Heterosexual sodomy is still a crime, but it is distinguished from its homosexual counterpart by a procedural privilege that has the effect of throwing a mantle of privacy over heterosexual fellatio, cunnilingus, and anal-genital contacts. What emerges as homosexual sodomy is conversely distinguished by its special exposure to discharge proceedings, to a stigmatizing discharge status, and thus to a peculiar publicity.

A further difference now becomes discernible: heterosexual and homosexual status are not only related to acts, they are *differently* related to acts. Discharge proceedings produce homosexual status as a one-for-one correspondence between homosexual acts and a personal type. But cross-sex sodomy is silent as to status. With respect to status, homosexual sodomy is metonymic, while cross-sex sodomy is not just opaque—it is semiotically inert.

Homosexual conduct and the "queen-for-a-day" exception. Even if same-sex conduct is singled out for particularly unfavorable treatment, it can be punished no matter who does it—that is, without reference to status. The New DOD Policy proposed to do just that. Although it allowed servicemembers being discharged for *saying they were gay* to stay in the military if they could prove that they had "no propensity" to engage in homosexual conduct, this defense was not available to servicemembers being processed for discharge for *engaging in same-sex conduct*. The Statute, unerring in its effort to distinguish homosexual and heterosexual persons and to extend special protections to the latter, invites servicemembers who have engaged in same-sex erotic conduct to establish the basis for their retention by proving (1) that they have no propensity to do precisely what they have done; (2) that their conduct is "a departure from [their] usual and customary behavior"; and (3) that their conduct is "not likely to recur." This and several other "propensity" provisions are considered together in chapter 3; here I focus more generally on the decision to reinstall a "queen-for-a-day" exception.

This decision recapitulates a long and feckless history of military regulation of same-sex erotic conduct. Perhaps the first and certainly an exemplary episode in this history was the World War I–era purge at the Newport Naval Training Station in Rhode Island. The Newport purge has been extensively documented in separate projects by Lawrence R. Murphy and George Chauncey, Jr., but a single, complex picture emerges from their work.

Naval officers at the training station became concerned about "immoral conditions" created by "sexual perverts," many of them in uniform (Chauncey 189; Murphy 15, 24). They began their investigations with a stable consensus that they could capture "perverts" by targeting a bright-line category of sexual acts: specifically, the activities of "cocksuckers and rectum receivers" (qtd. in Murphy 25). Investigators sent out to solicit sexual acts in Newport's lively homosexual subculture were instructed that they should "always [have] the other party do all the leading and commit all the acts" (qtd. in Murphy 21) and that they could not violate military law "if an act was committed upon them and they did not take any leading part" (qtd. in Murphy 30). Officials managing the early stages of the investigation, their investigators, military hearing boards, and finally courts-martial seem to have agreed that "perverts" constituted a distinctive personal type. Indeed, they agreed on that point with the local gay subculture, which described as "queer" those members who assumed "feminine" sexual roles (Chauncey 190–92) and who were understood to be taxonomically distinct from men who engaged in male-male sex while asserting masculine gender.

At the outset of the investigation, the Navy's conduct basis seemed well designed to capture perversion and protect normal masculinity. It would bypass the subculture's "husbands"—that is, men who "conformed to masculine gender norms [and were often] heterosexually married" and whom the "queers" recognized as part of "the gang" because of their "sexual, and sometimes explicitly romantic, interest in men" (Chauncey 192). It would also bypass men dubbed "trade" in the subculture—men who were "straight" in their self-perception and public identity and who were willing, sometimes eager, to engage in sex with the queers (Chauncey 195). And it would protect the decoys, whose job it was to engage in fellatio and anal sex with the targets of the purge and who seemed to display no concern that their involvement subjected them to suspicion of "perversion."

To official dismay, this acts-based dragnet captured not only perverts but others as well. Murphy reports that

Albert Veihl was imprisoned and subsequently court-martialed (and sentenced to twenty years) (Murphy 64) on his own confession that he had *been fellated by* one accused serviceman and *had anally penetrated* another. In confessing to these episodes, moreover, Veihl made the neophyte's excuse for them: "I never had an experience before and I didn't know what he was after"; "[It was] the first time in my life I ever did anything like this" (qtd. in Murphy 49). The very next day Lieutenant Commander Foster, then in charge of the Court of Inquiry, lost much of his enthusiasm for it: he warned a member of his court that "If they don't stop Arnold [one of the most active decoys] right away, they will hang the whole state of Rhode Island" (qtd. in Murphy 47). Husbands, trade, and young recruits with no habitual relationship to Newport's gay subculture were coming within reach of the investigation; and the univocal relationship between disfavored acts and disfavored persons was breaking down.

The purge became a political crisis, however, only after Navy officers and civilian officials turned its scopic glare on the civilian population, and in particular when they targeted a local Episcopal clergyman, Samuel Kent. Kent was the first victim of the purge to mount a meaningful defense. The strategy was to put crushing pressure on the Navy's assumption that receptive sexual activity univocally and uniquely indicated perverse personality. Kent's lawyers pushed for evidence that the decoys had engaged in homosexual acts *simpliciter* ("For the cause you were willing to go the limit?"), and they sought to locate perversion not in sexual role but in same-sex eroticism. As Chauncey reports, one decoy had trouble on cross-examination:

Q. You volunteered for this work?

A. Yes, sir.

Q. You knew what kind of work it was before you volunteered, didn't you?

A. Yes, sir.

Q. You knew it involved sucking and that sort of thing, didn't you?

A. I knew we had to deal with that, yes, sir.

Q. You knew it included sodomy and that sort of thing, didn't you?

A. Yes, sir.

Q. And you were quite willing to get into that sort of work?

A. I was willing to do it, yes, sir.

Q. And so willing that you volunteered for it, is that right?

A. Yes, sir. I volunteered for it, yes, sir.

Q. You knew it included buggering fellows, didn't you? (qtd. in Chauncey 198)

Another decoy sought to explain away his arousal: "Of course, a great deal of that was involuntary inasmuch as a man placing his hand on my penis would cause an erection and subsequent emission. That was uncontrollable on my part. . . . Probably I would have had it [the emission] when I got back in bed anyway. . . . It is a physiological fact" (qtd. in Chauncey 198). This testimony was probably crucial to Kent's acquittals in state and federal court, which became ominous signals to Navy officials that their neat alignment of personality, act, and desire was in the final stages of breaking down. In retreat from the resulting prospect that "many more men than the inner circle of queers and husbands would have to be investigated," Navy top brass repudiated the Newport investigation entirely and even offered clemency to some of its victims (Chauncey 198).

It would be a mistake to suppose that this outcome represented a liberatory social deconstruction. Kent's lawyers' strategy depended on an emerging consensus that decent men didn't do what the decoys did: "Have you a mother living? You think she should have been pleased at this?" they asked one decoy; "You had been a decent clean boy up to the time you enlisted in the navy? And never indulged in any of these practices?" they asked another (qtd. in Murphy 125, 132). Kent testified that, in response to one decoy's advances, he had remonstrated: "What are you doing, boy? Don't you know such a thing is wrong for you? . . . Keep clean and live a good life, and get married to a good girl" (qtd. in Murphy 141). As David Halperin concludes, the ecclesiastical polemics that grew out of Kent's defense, and that became an aggressive, and successful, political attack on the Navy's investigation, "considered any genital contact between two persons of the same sex to be a sign of pathological tendencies in *both* partners, no matter who did what to whom" (24; original emphasis). This was a change, but it was hardly an improvement.

After Newport, and perhaps in part because of it, military acts-based regulation of sexual-orientation identity has depended on the more familiar homo/hetero taxonomy of persons. But if the Newport fiasco should have taught anything to military regulators, it was that no single definition of prohibited acts can reliably exile just the right population of persons.

This is a lesson that acts-based regulation has never

finally learned. Instead, military anti-gay policy has repeatedly recoiled from acts to statuses and back again. Once the homo/hetero distinction overtook the description of persons, however, this recoil became formally simpler than the complex dissolution displayed in the Newport trials. Here's the cycle you see if you study the history of the regulations: strict acts-based policies eventually precipitate queen-for-a-day exceptions that turn on an assessment of homosexual or heterosexual personhood; the resulting exceptions are repeatedly found to offer low-level decision makers too much discretion and servicemembers too much room for strategic maneuver; they are narrowed or deleted and the resulting acts-based regulations are eventually found to be too harsh to heterosexual servicemembers; the exceptions are reinstated; found wanting again; and deleted again.

To follow just a few cycles of this post-Newport ambivalence, we can start in the midst of McCarthy era rigor, documented with wonderful vividness in an archival article by Allan Bérubé and John D'Emilio. Same-sex acts were dangerous to *anyone* during that time. But this draconian regime eventually led military psychologists to publish their deep distress at their inability to protect heterosexual soldiers from the life-destroying consequences of same-sex conduct (West, Doidge, and Williams). This ambivalence about apparently straight servicemembers who have engaged in homosexual conduct is richly demonstrated by constant revisions in the regulations applicable to them. The Army provided for psychiatric and medical examinations but warned that soldiers could be retained only if no "perverse tendencies" were found (Army Reg. 600–43 [Apr. 10, 1953]);

then it established the first exception for servicemembers who have engaged in "homosexual acts" in "an apparently isolated episode, stemming solely from immaturity, curiosity or intoxication" (Army Reg. 635–89 [July 15, 1966]); then it narrowed that permission by limiting it to cases involving "a single homosexual episode" (Army Reg. 635–89 [Oct. 1, 1968]); then it withdrew clemency altogether in revised regulations requiring discharge for a single act of homosexual sex (Army Reg. 635–100, Change No. 4 [Jan. 21, 1970]); and then it restored the permission for acts committed in an *apparently* isolated episode

(Army Reg. 635–200, Change No. 39 [Nov. 23, 1972]).

The pendulum was not yet still. In 1976 the Navy discharged James Miller under regulations, identical to those in the Army's 1970 rules, that made even a single homosexual act the grounds for mandatory separation (*Beller* 794, 802). Miller sued, and he presented a tough case for regulators who wished to offer status-based clemency to heterosexuals. In trial testimony, Miller repeatedly "denied being homosexual and expressed regret or repugnance at his acts," and a Senior Medical Officer concluded that "despite [Miller's] admitted homosexual episodes, he did not appear to be 'a homosexual'" (*Beller* 802 n. 9, 794). Not surprisingly, during the Miller litigation the Navy adopted the same queen-for-a-day exception that the Army had restored in 1972 (*Beller* 802 n. 9).

When Clinton proposed to eliminate the queen-for-a-day exception, and Congress refused to do so, the pendulum swung one more time. Against this historical backdrop Clinton's reform was strikingly gay-positive in that it did not merely narrow heterosexual-status exceptions; it eliminated them. Congress's swift retort protects heterosexual persons from any status-like consequences of their homosexual acts.

By restoring the queen-for-a-day exception, moreover, Congress steepened the subtle asymmetry I have already noted in the relationship that heterosexual status and homosexual status bear to same-sex erotic acts. Aspin's New DOD Policy extended the "no propensity" defense to servicemembers who have made self-identifying statements *but not* to those who have engaged in same-sex erotic acts. Underlying this pattern lay two implicit policy determinations, both of which depend on the supposition that there are true heterosexual and homosexual persons: first, that a true heterosexual might mistakenly (falsely) indicate by a statement that he was gay but that the false statement would be of little consequence to the smooth operation of the military because it could be corrected, as it were, by the servicemember's further evidence about his true (hetero)sexual orientation; and second, that the same person, if he engaged in a same-sex erotic act, did something uniquely and independently harmful to military effectiveness. The Statute intensifies the New DOD Policy's commitment to the notion of homo- and heterosexual personhood by altering the second of these premises: same-sex erotic acts are now deemed to be *differently* harmful depending on the *sexual status of the people who perform them*. A true heterosexual might mistakenly commit a same-sex erotic act, but it should not be deemed harmful to military essences *because it tells us nothing about him;* whereas a homosexual who engaged in the same act harms the military because his act provides an *unmediated view into his sexual self.* In its relationship to acts, homosexual identity has a transparency, a legibility, that heterosexual identity doesn't. The queen-for-a-day provision achieves the same effect as the elimination of "even-handed" enforcement: the "meaning" of conduct evidence, and the language for making inferences from act to status, are radically different for heterosexual persons and homosexual persons. This is not merely discrimination: it is meta-discrimination.

Homosexual Identification

"Don't ask" was the issue on which Clinton staked most, fought longest, had his single identifiable victory, and engaged in his most delusional refusals to acknowledge how meager his victory was and how massive were the accompanying losses. He achieved "don't ask" at the expense of "don't tell," and thus agreed to a pervasive and intimate system of status-based regulation.

One way to regulate conduct — not status — is to provide positive protection for identity statements by excluding them from the grounds for separation. President Clinton arrived in the White House with a clear understanding that protecting servicemembers from intrusive questioning about their sexual-orientation identities would be progress; what he did not anticipate was that between "don't ask" and "don't tell" lay ample territory for anti-gay status-based regulation.

First, "don't ask." The New DOD Policy, and Aspin's Guidelines explaining it, barred the armed services from asking servicemembers and new recruits whether they were gay. So do the Statute's Implementing Regulations. The MWG Report indicates how unwelcome "don't ask" must have been to military leaders. Its fundamental policy premise, that *"All homosexuality is incompatible with military service,"* would have justified vigorous and invasive inquisitorial efforts. And its grand concession — "don't ask" new recruits (but do ask servicemembers once they're in uniform) — indicates that the New DOD Policy's across-the-board "don't ask" provision was a hard-won White House achievement. Moreover, the "don't ask" principle was Clinton's only gesture in the direction of acts-based regulation that the Statute didn't positively overrule. The "don't ask" provisions represent the high-water mark of Clinton's reforms.

But this bar on accession and in-service questioning is more ephemeral and less meaningful than it may initially appear. Congress refused to *require* "don't ask" in the Statute, implicitly delegating to the Department of Defense the decision whether to bar direct identity questioning. Moreover, Congress clearly indicated that its silence was to be construed to empower future administrations to strip "don't ask" from military regulations. In a "Sense of Congress" statement approved along with the bill that ultimately became codified as the Statute, Congress expressed its intention that, "if the Secretary determines that it is necessary to do so to effectuate the policy set forth" in the Statute's findings, the Statute must be construed to allow the Secretary of Defense to reinstate "questioning concerning homosexuality" in the accession process. The Secretary of Defense could simply reinstate "such questions" as were asked before the Clinton administration called a halt to accession questioning about homosexual orientation — an invitation which, if accepted, would reintroduce frontal questioning about sexual orientation.

A "Sense of Congress" statement is not presented to the president for his signature, and is therefore not codified with the Statute as "law." But it is published with the Public Laws record of congressional actions, where it offers a gloss on Congress's intent in passing the Statute. This device thus allowed Clinton to profess that he would enforce "don't ask" and Congress to assure itself that his choice to do so as a matter of regulation could be swiftly reversed by a subsequent administration.

Moreover, the entire subsequent history of "don't ask" indicates that Clinton's goal in this part of his struggle with Congress was the appearance, not the reality, of a "don't ask" reform. First, the Implementing Regulations —which are entirely within the control of the executive branch—warn that they provide guidance to commanders but do not create any substantive or procedural rights (DODD2/a G and DODD3/a G; DODD2/a D.3 and DODD3/a D.3). If "don't ask" is a right, it is a right without a remedy. Servicemembers who have been asked have no recourse.

Second, if "don't ask" confers a right, it is frequently honored only in the breach. One servicemember was asked, "I won't ask you whether you're gay, but if I did, what would you say?" Other questions are less cagey: the Statute did not prevent an officer from asking one servicemember, "Are you a fucking faggot?" (Miles 65).[3]

Third, military officials can refrain from asking, "Are you gay?" and yet pose a vast range of perfectly legitimate questions about sexual orientation identity. This problem is illustrated by the discharge proceedings of Army Reserve Sergeant Steven Spencer. When Spencer came out in late July 1993, the Army promptly initiated an investigation preparatory to separating him from service. Pursuing that investigation *within the limits set by the New DOD Policy* (as well as those set by the then-still-to-be-promulgated Implementing Regulations), the Army was able to ask all these questions without once asking Spencer whether he was gay: "[H]ave you ever stated that you are homosexual? Have you ever stated that you are bisexual? Have you engaged in, attempted to engage in, or solicited another to engage in a homosexual act or acts? Do you intend to engage in homosexual acts in the future? Are you married to or have you attempted to marry a person know [*sic*] to be of the same biological sex 'as evidenced by the external anatomy of the persons involved'? . . . [Do] you have a propensity or intent to commit homosexual acts, now or in the future?" (Army1).

And fourth, "don't ask" is only the beginning of life under "don't tell." "Don't ask" and "don't pursue" (DODI2) narrow somewhat the grounds upon which commanders can initiate investigations of servicemembers' sexuality: they can't directly ask a servicemember whether he is gay, and they can't begin a campaign of surveillance based on unreliable information. But they can initiate investigations if they gain access to the fruits of "asking" by other branches of government; if they receive any evidence of conduct that manifests a propensity to engage in homosexual conduct; and if they receive evidence that a servicemember has stated, privately or publicly, that he or she is gay, lesbian, or bisexual. If this information remains unsupplemented but is deemed to be "credible," moreover, commanders have the power to initiate discharge proceedings in which the servicemember must be discharged unless he or she is able to prove that he or she lacks any propensity to engage in homosexual conduct.

Then, of course, there's "don't tell" itself. Its reach is remarkable. Marine Corporal Kevin Blaesing was processed for discharge because he told a Navy psychologist that he wondered whether he might be gay, and asked her about sexual orientation ("Don't Ask"; Raddatz). The new policy apparently provides for the discharge of servicemembers who disclose anything about their relationship to homosexuality—even a desire for information about it—*to anyone*—even a single individual in the apparent privacy of a therapeutic relationship.

At the other end of the private-public spectrum, "don't tell" gags servicemembers' explicitly political speech. Sergeant Spencer was asked the questions quoted above because he came out as gay when he joined a lawsuit challenging the Old DOD Policy and the Interim Policy (CP2). At that time the other plaintiffs involved in the litigation remained closeted, and the suit was styled *Doe v. Perry* to protect the plaintiffs from the operation of the policy they challenged, *so that* they could challenge it. Having fired a warning shot in the form of the Spencer discharge proceedings, the Department of Defense refused, despite repeated and explicit requests from the plaintiffs' attorney, to guarantee that any of the plaintiffs would be preserved from discharge based on their participation in the litigation. Five plaintiffs nevertheless came out as gay or lesbian in the complaint, but the lead plaintiff, Army Reserve Lieutenant Colonel Janet Able, remains covered by a pseudonym.

To be sure, the *Able* plaintiffs could have filed suit challenging the Statute without "telling." But doing so would have exposed them to risky litigation about their standing to sue, without protecting them from discharge proceedings initiated on the ground that joining the complaint was conduct that a reasonable person would construe to manifest a propensity to engage in homosexual conduct. And they would have foregone an important aspect of bringing their challenge to the public forum of the federal district court: the opportunity to display to the court the actual human beings upon whom the Statute stood ready to operate. It is hard to imagine a clearer instance of coming out as political speech.[4]

"Don't tell," then, stripped away most of the umbrella of protection Clinton claimed that he had secured with "don't ask." Even worse, "don't tell" caused yet another collapse in the White House's vaunted distinction between conduct and status. Clinton came to the bargaining table in July willing to agree to "don't tell" as long as servicemembers could "tell" discreetly, privately, and with a specific proviso that they did not intend to engage in actual misconduct. As he said at his July 19, 1993, press conference, "Under this policy . . . a person can say 'I am a homosexual but I am going to strictly adhere to the code of conduct.' " He remained so convinced that he had put a status/conduct distinction into effect that, in a weird, protracted display of political and discursive somnambulism, he continued to insist that he had secured this proviso up to the very day that Aspin announced the New DOD Policy — which provided no such protection and instead classified any act of "telling" *as* "homosexual conduct"! Clinton's delusional view of his accomplishment on behalf of gay men and lesbians caused "considerable confusion" (Doe) and sharp indignation among his opponents in the negotiations (*Crossfire;* Cong.6), and he was quick to correct his mistake in a speech delivered to the National Defense University at Fort McNair later the same day (WH4).

Clinton seems to have forgotten that, just days earlier, a senior administration official had displayed the disintegration of his proviso, and of the status/conduct distinction which it would have done something to honor, under relentless political pressure to put a bar on public gay identity *as a species of conduct.* This official — unnamed in on-line press conference transcripts — claimed that the Joint Chiefs and the White House had agreed on a revised policy providing that a single act of coming out, even on network television, would not trigger an investigation as long as the servicemember added the proviso, "but while I'm in the military I'm not going to engage in any unpermitted conduct" (WH3). But under raucous questioning from the press the spokesperson soon conceded that a servicemember whose public identity thus painstakingly excluded conduct could nevertheless be processed for discharge if she came out more than once, or if she came out once and military officials *heard about it from more than one source* (WH3).

To read this as regulation of conduct, as the New DOD Policy asks us to do, requires a concept of distinct *acts of being known to be gay.* Where acts of being known to be gay are the "conduct" that a serviceperson may commit, the status/conduct distinction is clearly in some difficulty. Indeed, the very idea that a gay servicemember and a straight one are distinct types of person is in trouble. The 1993 revisions, once again, can be fully understood only if we take into account their discursive as well as their material effects.

The theory of speech acts set out by J. L. Austin in *How to Do Things with Words* is very helpful here. This posthumous publication includes Austin's James Lectures delivered at Harvard University in 1955. Austin began his lectures with the proposition that, while it is "the business" of some utterances "to 'describe' some state of affairs, or to 'state some fact,' which [they] must do either truly or falsely"—utterances he dubbed *constative*—others do an action. These he dubbed *performatives* (Austin 3, 4–7). Austin's theory would draw our attention to the way in which the 1993 revisions govern not only the referential content of a servicemember's statement, "I am gay"—her status—but also the social function of that utterance as a speech act, an act of communication that involves both a sender and a receiver. As Austin first set it out, moreover, his theory would suggest that the former was distinct from the latter; that the constative and performative aspects of coming out statements—and thus, implicitly, their status and conduct implications—were distinct.

But Austin rapidly deconstructed his distinction in Lecture I between constatives and performatives as alternate classes of utterances, and devoted his work from Lecture V on to puzzling out the consequences of his later realization that many utterances are both falsifiable descriptions of extralinguistic states of affairs *and* "the doing of . . . action[s]" (53 ff.). If Austin's theory applies to coming-out statements as they are understood under the 1993 revisions, saying "I am gay" is both constative and performative at the same time. Such an utterance announces a state of affairs *and* functions as a mode of social action. It involves status *and* conduct.

Moreover, as a performative, the statement *includes, as*

part of its content, its reception in the public sphere of its audiences. It must have been with some intuition of Austin's later understanding of speech acts that an unnamed "senior Administration official" advocated "don't tell" because it would prevent the latter: "we . . . want to avoid giving license for someone to go up to their commanding officer and say, 'I'm gay, and I want everyone here to know that'" (Friedman, "Clinton Is Said to Accept"). To track Austin further, the 1993 revisions regard the speech act of coming out to include not only the illocutionary force imparted by its maker's social performance

in making it, but the perlocutionary force imparted by its audience in reacting to it (98–100, 109–20). If the perlocutionary uptake of coming-out statements is an intrinsic part of their operation as speech-as-conduct, the "conduct" regulated by the new military anti-gay policy is *the complete social regime of its ascription.*

"Don't tell" implicitly breaks down the status/conduct distinction and rejects the view that homosexual conduct (and thus homosexual status) belong to homosexuals alone. What "don't ask" leaves implicit, the propensity clauses make explicit.

3   But Everyone Agrees on the
Propensity Clauses

The most striking novelty of the 1993 revisions, shared by the New DOD Policy and the Statute, is the regulation of persons with a *propensity* to engage in homosexual conduct. Both the New DOD Policy and the Statute define "homosexual acts" to include "bodily contact which a reasonable person would understand to demonstrate *a propensity* or intent to engage in" an erotic, same-sex bodily contact. Coming-out statements and conduct short of sodomy are grounds for discharge inasmuch as they demonstrate intent or *propensity*. Moreover, under the Statute in all cases, and under the New DOD Policy in cases initiated by a servicemember's statement of homosexual identity, the servicemember can stay in the military only if she shows that she in fact lacks *a propensity* to engage in homosexual conduct.

All of these provisions are new. The term "propensity" appeared only once in the Old DOD Policy, in a preamble that justified the provisions which followed in part by disparaging the presence in "the military environment of persons . . . who, by their statements, demonstrate a propensity to engage in homosexual conduct." But the

Old DOD Policy's actual separation procedures made no further use of the concept of propensity, and focused instead on desire, intention, and the status description "*a homosexual.*" Propensity was not even in part a basis for exclusion or separation.

In what sense does the introduction of "propensity" shift regulatory attention from status to conduct? The Statute's preamble suggests an answer, in the form of a series of congressional "findings" insisting that Congress seeks to *reduce the risk* of same-sex conduct. For example: "The armed forces must maintain personnel policies that exclude persons whose presence in the armed forces would create an unacceptable risk to the armed forces' high standards of morale, good order and discipline, and unit cohesion that are the essence of military capability."

The logic seems to be this. First, homosexual conduct when it occurs is harmful to "the armed forces' high standards of morale, good order and discipline, and unit cohesion." Second, these features of military life are "the essence of military capability"; harming them is very bad. Therefore, third, the military must *prevent* actual harm by reducing the *risk* of homosexual conduct: "persons who demonstrate a propensity or intent to engage in homosexual acts . . . create an unacceptable risk" to the very "essence of military capability" and should be subject to exclusion. According to this logic, detecting people with a propensity is merely a prudent way of identifying servicemembers who are likely to engage in harmful conduct and getting them out of the military before they can actually harm its essences.

I will call this the actuarial model of sexual orientation

propensity.[1] It resembles the social description of insurers who, for example, might require higher insurance premiums from policyholders who live in cities with high rates of auto fatalities than from those living elsewhere. In the actuarial context, the reason for imposing special burdens on some people and not others is not any assessment of their character or personality, but the bureaucratic management of an adventitious, heuristic category that allows predictions about where in a population certain socially costly events are likely to occur. No special metaphysical confidence is attached to the differentiation between cities (or, to the extent propensity is an actuarial concept, among sexual-orientation identities). Instead, actuarial categories are merely well-correlated with costly outcomes, and could be abandoned if better correlative categories were to be developed. Nor are individual members of these categories subjected to disadvantage with any special epistemic confidence. Instead, special burdens are imposed on them because the correlation supports not a certainty but an increased probability that they, personally, will produce a costly outcome. Everything about the correlative social category is (supposedly) tentative, instrumental, heuristic, artificial, technical, and disposable: the focus of the analysis is on the bad event—automobile accidents, same-sex sodomy—that the regulator is (it is assumed) entitled to avoid.

In statement cases, the assignment of an actuarial propensity produces a conduct basis for separation without any need for evidence of actual conduct or of its conventional substitute, an ascription of homosexual personhood. For defenders of the 1993 revisions, the constitutional upsides of this model of propensity are substantial.

First, by providing a conduct basis for discrimination against an entire social class, the actuarial model of propensity fortifies the claim that *Hardwick* forecloses heightened equal protection scrutiny of government's anti-gay policies.

Second, it describes anti-gay discrimination in a way that precisely answers the questions asked in off-the-shelf rational-basis review. Where no heightened scrutiny is required, the Supreme Court has held, government is allowed to address social problems in ways that are merely rational: it can tackle them one step at a time, can indulge in overinclusive and underinclusive approaches as long as the bad fit is not wildly disproportionate or indicative of social prejudices, and can expect federal courts to take into account the administrative difficulties involved (*Cleburne; Heller; Williamson v. Lee Optical*). If the government offered automobile insurance it could impose higher rates on all the inhabitants of a city that showed a higher-than-average accident rate; similarly, the argument goes, it can determine that people who say they are gay pose a higher-than-average risk of homosexual sodomy, and can be eliminated from the armed services as part of an effort to reduce the incidence of that conduct.

Third, the rebuttable presumption of a propensity provides the basis for a new defense against First Amendment challenges. Attorney General Janet Reno specifically warned that a policy allowing for discharge on the basis of coming-out "statements" alone would be vulnerable to First Amendment free-speech challenges, and approved of the procedural device allowing a servicemember who has made a gay-identifying statement to rebut the resulting presumption that he or she has a propensity to commit homosexual *acts.* In a memorandum from Reno to Clinton, dated July 19, 1993, and distributed that day along with the New DOD Policy to congressional committees, Reno opined that this "meaningful opportunity to rebut the presumption flowing from statements of homosexuality" renders "the Department of Justice . . . better able to argue that the policy is not directed at speech or expression itself" but at conduct.[2]

Fourth, the actuarial model of propensity offers rhetorical advantages to anti-gay apologists. By implicitly disavowing any belief in essentially homosexual persons, the actuarial model of propensity works to disable rights rhetoric, to avoid scrutiny for fairness, and generally to evade moral evaluation. Efficiency rather than fairness provides the justification for regulating harmful conduct before the fact rather than after it. Bureaucratic convenience is invoked to justify separating some servicemembers who, though they are indeed homosexual, would never themselves engage in disparaged conduct. The actuarial model allows defenders of military anti-gay policy to adopt a benign tone which purportedly justifies, in turn, their claim to work from a position beyond moral critique: far from pursuing an anti-gay social agenda, they are merely setting up a special-purpose regulatory category with no necessary relationship to real social groups or individuals. Since such a nominalist approach can hardly express animus toward any real social group, its proponents can claim that their project is non-normative or even *a*normative. Conjoined with the related claim that the military itself (like a life insurance scheme) is a special-purpose social aggregation immune from most moral constraints applicable to other civic actors, the actuarial model supports the claim, often heard during the 1993 debates, that military sexuality policy belongs to military expertise and was of no moment to civil society.

And fifth, just as the actuarial model of propensity allows anti-gay apologists to evade moral criticism, it locks pro-gay litigators into an apparently inescapable double bind. While it might have been plausible for them to claim that a servicemember should not be discharged on the basis of conduct for which there is no proof, it is quite a different matter to claim that his or her self-description as "homosexual" refers to "status" alone and has *nothing to do with* homosexual conduct. Navy midshipman Joseph Steffan's lawyers walked directly into this trap, persistently asserting that their client's statement-based separation implicated only his "status" as a homosexual and was conceptually as well as actually devoid of a basis in conduct. But to deny a conceptual, indeed a statistically noticeable empirical relationship between same-sex erotic contacts and the social group of self-described gay men, lesbians, and bisexuals is not just conceptually absurd and empirically heroic; it contradicts the persistent tenets of gay, lesbian, bisexual, and queer political movements, which have sought to endorse, not abandon, same-sex eroticism. The actuarial model of propensity sets up the double bind that judges cinched whenever they asked plaintiffs why they sought protection only for celibate homosexuals or when, in a particularly devastating move, they noted that Lambda Legal Defense and Education Fund had submitted amicus briefs not only in *Steffan* but in *Hardwick* as well, and that in the earlier case it had argued that sodomy was a necessary element of gay life. The D.C. Circuit Court Court of Appeals, rejecting Steffan's claim, observed: "Lambda, the gay rights organization representing Steffan, appeared as amicus in Bowers. Arguing against the constitutionality of criminalizing homosexual sodomy, it asserted that the 'regulation of same sex behavior constitutes the total prohibition of an entire way of life' because homosexuality is inexorably intertwined with 'homosexual conduct'" *(Steffan E* 690 n. 11, quoting CP4 23 n. 28; see also *Richenberg C* 262).

The actuarial model of propensity tempts pro-gay advocates into this double bind. Whenever pro-gay challenges to military anti-gay policy depend on denying a normative, conceptual, and statistical relationship between homosexual self-identification and same-sex erotic conduct, they contradict most gay-affirmative rhetoric since Stonewall, and seek constitutional vindication only for a gay and lesbian movement that is, at least in its public self-representations, sexually inert. That is not the gay and lesbian movement we have, as even federal judges know.

Of course, neither are apologists for the 1993 revisions to be trusted when they claim that the propensity provisions regulate conduct and not status. Those provisions, far from forswearing regulation of persons, are like all the provisions examined in chapter 2 in that they pursue it with new subtlety. After all, dictionaries of common language define a "propensity" as an inner, intrinsic, even natural or innate characteristic of individual persons, animals, and plants—a "bent," to emphasize a synonym that is particularly resonant here—that directs them to particular forms of action.[3] As I show in some detail below, before the actuarial model of propensity emerged in military anti-gay policy, Department of Justice (DOJ) lawyers consistently treated the term "propensity" in the justificatory preamble of the Old DOD Policy as a homonym of "proclivity." Army General H. Norman Schwarzkopf testified before the Senate Armed Services Committee that the Old DOD Policy should not be altered because "homosexuals, by definition, are individuals who have an *established predilection* for violating the Uniform Code of Military Justice through the commission of sodomy. Exclusion of homosexuals from military service is a means of precluding military service by a group of individuals who have a natural proclivity to commit criminal acts" (Cong.2 599; emphasis added). This gloss on the Old DOD Policy's use of "propensity" construes it as a criminal character flaw — an *intrinsic* psychological or physical feature — lodged in every individual member of the group Schwarzkopf seeks to exclude.

I will call this the *psychometric* model of propensity. It attributes a pathological personal trait to each individual homosexual. It thus contradicts every important feature of the actuarial model: it is realist about the social description it proposes, boldly confident that the bearers of that description are or will inevitably be involved in criminal sexual conduct, and vigorously normative.

The psychometric model of propensity makes claims about personhood — and personhood, we have already seen, was the most substantial meaning of "status" in the 1993 debates. If the actuarial model of propensity emphasizes conduct, then, the psychometric model emphasizes status. The claim that the 1993 revisions shifted regulatory attention from status to conduct thus depends on a claim that the propensity clauses adhere to the actuarial, and not the psychometric, model of propensity.

But they do no such thing. The psychometric model

of homosexual propensity is a hidden premise of the actuarial model. Consider an important conceptual difference between the insurance example given above and military anti-gay policy. When an insurance company predicts that the inhabitants of Anycity will have a higher-than-average rate of automobile accidents, it invokes a territorial and social boundary set for reasons unrelated to the project of spreading the risk of automobile accidents. But when the military predicts that self-described homosexuals will commit homosexual sodomy unacceptably often, it invokes a category of persons that has been developed precisely to make sense of its category of acts. A suppressed reference to psychometric concepts thus supports General Schwarzkopf's observation that self-described homosexuals are predisposed to violate the UCMJ ban on sodomy. By eliding the fact that the UCMJ bans *heterosexual* fellatio, *heterosexual* cunnilingus, and *heterosexual* anal intercourse, Schwarzkopf excludes self-identified heterosexuals from his purportedly acts-based rationale. The conduct he seeks to eliminate is predefined by a suppressed reference to the persons he wishes to exclude (and, more covertly, those he wishes to protect): his very definition of the act depends on a definition (and social ordering) of persons.

The actuarial model of homosexual propensity thus conceptually entails the psychometric model of homosexual propensity. The 1993 revisions played out this conceptual relationship, both in the process of inscribing propensity into the New DOD Policy and in the military's practices of enforcing the new Statute.

We know a lot about who introduced, fought for, and resisted the various provisions of the New DOD Policy and
the Statute. Much of the New DOD Policy comes directly,
even verbatim, from a Military Working Group (MWG) Report commissioned by Aspin but written by military top
brass. (It is inconceivable that anything in the MWG Report contradicted the wishes of the Joint Chiefs.) This
report stated the basic premise that "*all homosexuality is
incompatible with military service*"; it proposed to tolerate
66   only entirely secretive homosexual orientation. We know
from chapter 2 that the Statute's finding that homosexuality is incompatible with military service comes from the
MWG Report. The MWG Report also contributed the New
DOD Policy's rule that servicemembers would be separated for "homosexual conduct," and its inclusion within
that rule of homosexual acts, coming-out statements, and
an actual or attempted homosexual marriage. The New
DOD Policy's "don't ask" language first emerged in the
MWG Report, where it signals the Joint Chiefs' sole compromise with the White House; Congress, as we know
from chapter 2, undid the deal, and left "don't ask" out
of the Statute. We also know from chapter 2 that Clinton
pushed for the New DOD Policy's "even-handed enforcement" language, and that Congress deleted it, and reintroduced the queen-for-a-day exception, in the Statute.
Clearly the Joint Chiefs and congressional proponents
of a strongly anti-gay policy did almost all the enduring
legislative draftsmanship of the 1993 revisions.[4]

It is all the more intriguing, then, to discover that
the true novelty of the 1993 revisions—the propensity

clauses—were not in the MWG Report, were in the New DOD Policy, and slid through the process seemingly without authors, proponents, or opponents. Who introduced the New DOD Policy's prohibition of statements that "demonstrate a *propensity to engage in homosexual acts*"? Whose fingerprints are on the New DOD Policy's and the Statute's related prohibition of conduct "which *a reasonable person would understand to demonstrate a propensity or intent to engage in homosexual acts*"? And who thought up the New DOD Policy's last great novelty, carried forward by the Statute: servicemembers who come out as gay, and under the Statute servicemembers who have engaged in homosexual acts as well, can stay in uniform if they can show that they "do[] not engage in homosexual acts *and do[ ] not have a propensity or intent to do so*"? The propensity cluster, which is the truly remarkable novelty of the 1993 revisions, was transposed into the Statute virtually verbatim from the New DOD Policy. But who wrote it into the New DOD Policy?

The propensity cluster can't be attributed to any of the usual suspects. Though military leaders had a pervasive impact on the text of the New DOD Policy, I've been unable to find any evidence that they introduced the propensity cluster. The word "propensity" does not appear in the MWG Report. If anything, the MWG's proposed policy set forth far less capacious conduct grounds: whereas it would have based discharge on statements of gay identity and "homosexual conduct" *simpliciter,* Aspin's policy went on to define conduct almost as broadly as possible, to include any contact "which a reasonable person would understand to demonstrate a propensity to engage in homosexual acts."

Nor have I found anything to support an attribution of these innovations to the Clinton White House, which either did not support or did not understand them. On July 19, 1993, the same day that Aspin was presenting the New DOD Policy to Congress, Clinton made a speech to the National Defense University at Fort McNair in which he insisted that the new policy sanctions "conduct, not . . . sexual orientation," and that it therefore provided to any servicemember who stated he or she was gay an opportunity to rebut the "presumption that he or she *intends to engage in prohibited conduct*" (WH4). Wrong on

both counts: the presumption of an intent *and propensity* to engage not merely in UCMJ-prohibited conduct but in *homosexual acts* is far more difficult to rebut than the one Clinton described, and substantially defeats his claim that he was promulgating mere conduct regulation.

My reading of the public record indicates that the absolute public debut of propensity as a basis for discharge in the public debates about the 1993 revisions was Senator Sam Nunn's July 16 speech on the floor of the Senate (Cong.4). By that time Nunn was widely recognized to be the leader of senatorial pro-ban efforts. But I don't believe Nunn, acting alone, was then in a position to make textual changes as substantial as those required to introduce the three elements of the propensity cluster. At this point in the process Nunn was manifestly not getting what he wanted. On July 16 Nunn explicitly threatened to legislate if he did not like the imminently forthcoming New DOD Policy. He promised to hold out for five "principles" — none of which got into Aspin's proposal because of Nunn's intervention. The five "principles" were the following:

1. military service is a unique calling which has no counterpart in civilian society;
2. the foundation of combat capability is unit cohesion;
3. military personnel policies must facilitate the assignment and the worldwide deployment of service members who frequently must live and work under close conditions affording minimal privacy;
4. the presence in military units of persons who, by their acts or by their statements demonstrate a propensity to engage in homosexual acts, would cause an unacceptable risk to the high standards of morale, good order, and discipline, and unit cohesion that are absolutely essential to effective combat capability;
5. while DOD policies on investigations may be subject to commonsense limitations . . . , these policies should not preclude investigations based upon any information relevant to an administrative or disciplinary proceeding. (Cong.4)

If anything, the New DOD Policy indicates the Clinton administration's near-total refusal to accede to Nunn's demands. The "unit cohesion" rationale (2) owes nothing to Nunn: it appears indiscriminately in all important versions of the 1993 revisions. Here Nunn was merely demanding what he was sure to get. He had to wait until October, when he surely had a major role in drafting the Statute, to inscribe the "military uniqueness" and "worldwide deployment" rationales (1 and 3) into public law, and to render the "privacy" rationale (3) unambiguously anti-gay. His attack on "don't ask" (5) was the opening salvo in a battle he will not finally win until a new president appoints a new secretary of defense willing to take advantage of the Statute's "Sense of Congress" statement permitting the military to ask at will. The propensity language Nunn advocated (4) stands alone as the single Nunn ultimatum that was met in the New DOD Policy.

What explains Aspin's accession to Nunn's demand for propensity language, given his otherwise striking willingness to frustrate him? The record best supports the following answer. When Nunn made his speech, Aspin was one day into his four-day delay in producing the New DOD Policy. Nunn's speech was only one indication that the key players intensified their involvement during this period. It was at this time that the pro-gay Campaign for Military Service made a bid for inclusion which so angered the White House that Clinton's advisors severed this sole link with gay constituencies (Burr). And it was during this period that press reports first noted the active involvement of Attorney General Janet Reno in the negotiations.

By July 15, the due date of Aspin's proposed policy, the chief unresolved issue was "don't tell"—that is, whether the military could discharge servicemembers who had engaged in no provable same-sex erotic acts but who stated that they were gay. Reno was reported to have warned Clinton aides that the "policy could be hard to defend in court" against equal protection and free speech challenges if it "went too far in prohibiting homosexuals from saying things that heterosexual soldiers were free to express" (Friedman, "Clinton Is Said to Accept"). Toward the close of the negotiations, Reno wrote her memorandum dated July 19, 1993, and distributed by Aspin that same day as an attachment to copies of the New DOD Policy. It opined that a military policy focused on conduct rather than status—on homosexual acts rather than "an unmanifested orientation"—would "appear fairer, more even-handed, and conduct-based, and thus easier to defend." The Reno Memo pronounces a special benediction on the provision allowing servicemembers who came out as gay or lesbian to stay in service if they *could demonstrate their lack of a propensity,* calling it the "most important improvement" in the New DOD Policy.

Reno may well have been the player who had the propensity brainstorm and carried the propensity language to the bargaining table, but I doubt it. Instead, her appearance in the negotiations is probably belated evidence of the involvement of the lawyers: career attorneys in the DOJ and the DOD who had developed almost every part of the propensity cluster during years of defending the Old DOD Policy from constitutional attack. Indeed, "Code 34," the Navy's team of appellate litigators, brags in a memorandum about implementing the Statute that "Code 34 provided significant input to the drafters of the 'new' policy and the implementing regulations" (Navy1).

The strongest evidence of this genealogy is in the public record: virtually every word of the three propensity elements is vividly anticipated in the DOJ's strategy for defending the Old DOD Policy after *Hardwick.* Step by step, from case to case and from one judicial response to the next, the DOJ gradually developed the propensity basis and the rebuttable presumption of a propensity not merely because they approximated *Hardwick's* focus on conduct, but because they mimicked its management of the status/conduct distinction. If *Hardwick* put the Supreme Court's imprimatur on the use of that distinction not as an opposition but as a diacritics, the DOJ's defensive rearticulations of the Old DOD Policy eventually translated *Hardwick's* achievement into a procedural recipe for the 1993 revisions. The propensity cluster has its origins not in any progressive reformism Clinton or Reno brought with them to their new jobs, but in the DOJ's historical role as the constitutional defender of a status-based military anti-gay policy.

72 *From Hardwick to the propensity concept. Hardwick* was a watershed in the DOJ's strategy for defending military anti-gay policy. Before *Hardwick* was handed down in 1986, the military had developed two independent grounds for sexuality-based separations: homosexual conduct *or* homosexual personality. At least since the early part of this century the military services when seeking to discharge gay personnel pressed hard for admissions and accusations of sexual conduct. The narrative histories of military anti-gay enforcement compiled by Allan Bérubé, John D'Emilio, and Randy Shilts amply document their method: if servicemembers rumored to be homosexual or to have engaged in conduct wouldn't immediately confess to conduct on the basis of which they could be separated, military investigators would hang the twin Damocles's swords of court-martial and dishonorable discharge over their heads while subjecting them and all their associates to prolonged questioning about the details of their sexual lives.

Though this strategy did allow the military to convert many statement cases into conduct cases, it had the defects of its virtues: its inquisitorial style offended many civilians, and, inasmuch as it explicitly sought self-incriminating statements, it eventually emboldened servicemembers to insist on legal representation. Both defects emerged in litigation in 1982, when a federal district court held that the Army could not discharge Sergeant Perry Watkins for saying he was gay and attached to its opinion a transcript of his predischarge interrogation (*Watkins A* 225–32). This unusual appendix demonstrates not only the confident thuggery of the inquisitors, and not only the effectiveness of an attorney in frustrating them, but also, by its mere publication, at least a soupçon of judicial indignation.

The alternative, widely used between World War II and the promulgation of the Old DOD Policy, was to base discharges on a servicemember's admission of "homosexual tendencies" or homosexual personality, even if no evidence of conduct was forthcoming. By 1970, this psychometric emphasis appeared in Army regulations requiring separation of any servicemember who "evidences homosexual tendencies, desire, or interest" even if he or she "is without overt homosexual acts" (Army Reg. 635–212; later Army Reg. 135–178, Chap. 7–5b(6)). The first round of the Army's proceedings against Miriam Ben-Shalom tested this language. Though the Army made an initial feint in the direction of separating her for her alleged "homosexual activities" (of which it had, apparently, no evidence at all), it promptly switched course and justified her exclusion solely on the grounds of her frank description of herself as a lesbian (*Ben-Shalom I* 969). When Ben-Shalom sued to challenge her discharge, the Army sought a ruling that the Constitution did not prevent it from determining that psychometric homosexual "status" alone, without conduct, was adverse to military purposes and an appropriate grounds for discharge: "[T]he government has steadfastly maintained [that] the petitioner lost her job simply because of what she is—a homosexual" (*Ben-Shalom I* 975).

The Army lost this first stage of its litigation with Ben-Shalom, an early warning that statement separations would appear to trial judges to be improperly based on "status." The warning must have been particularly unwelcome to lawyers charged with defending the then-new **74** Old DOD Policy, which made self-identifying statements an independent ground for separation. When the *Hardwick* decision was handed down in 1986, however, new defensive possibilities emerged. The government wanted to invoke *Hardwick* not only in sodomy-based discharges but in statement cases as well. As it struggled to articulate a conduct basis for statement cases, it gradually adopted *Hardwick's* management of conduct and status as mutually defining, mutually probative elements of homosexual identity.

Translating this discourse into actual separation procedures took time. The successive rationales for statement-based cases went from

(1) imputing actual sodomy as a matter of law; to
(2) inducing the servicemember to make a factual concession that he had engaged in sodomy; to
(3) imputing a propensity to commit sodomy as a matter of law; to
(4) inducing the servicemember to make a fac-

tual concession that he himself has a propensity
to engage in sodomy.

These successive translations of the status/conduct relationship incorporate status as a hidden but defining term
of conduct.

Imputing actual sodomy as a matter of law. It was one
thing for the D.C. Circuit to hold, in *Padula v. Webster*, that
Hardwick foreclosed serious equal-protection scrutiny of
anti-gay discrimination because sodomy was the "behavior that defined the class" seeking protection (103). It
was quite another for the Navy to find as a fact that, because Joseph Steffan stated that he was gay, he personally
had violated the UCMJ criminal sodomy statute. The *Padula* logic was available as a reason to reject gay plaintiffs'
claims that homosexuals need extra judicial protection
under the equal protection clause: after all, if *Hardwick*
made membership in the class a proper subject of criminal punishment, how could courts interfere with mere
civil discrimination against it? The Navy's finding went
well beyond that, to attribute *actual* sodomy to a class
member.

Steffan was just about to graduate from the Naval
Academy in 1987 when his superiors asked him about his
sexual orientation and he replied that he was gay. He was
pressured to resign, and did so on the basis of a record
entirely devoid of evidence that he had engaged in any
same-sex conduct. A report by the Brigade Military Performance Board concluded that he "was, in fact, homosexual" and recommended his discharge on that ground
alone (CP9 5). *On that basis,* the Naval Investigative Service (NIS) went on in its official report of the affair to

find that "inquiry had resulted in a determination that [Steffan] is in violation of Article 125," the section of the Uniform Code of Military Justice criminalizing sodomy (CP9 10).

This tactic had the advantage that it imputed actual sodomitical deeds to Steffan himself. It also had the grave disadvantage that it rested a government action destroying a young man's career and expelling him from college just weeks before his graduation on the ground that he personally had engaged in felonious conduct that had never been alleged against him, proven, or adjudicated. If discharges were to be based on sodomitical misconduct, some other way of linking servicemembers with it needed to be worked out.

The *Padula* court's determination that sodomy defines the class of homosexuals was the legal conclusion of an appellate court; extending that attribution to a particular self-described gay man appeared at first to be a *factual* question requiring some record basis. But in many statement cases — and especially in the ones gay litigators emphasized after *Hardwick* — facts about homosexual contacts were hard to come by. In subsequent phases of the *Steffan* case, and in other cases, DOJ lawyers undertook to find a better way of attaching the legal opprobrium and vulnerability that the *Hardwick* Court heaped on homosexual sodomy to the *particular individuals* who had been discharged. The goal was to infuse a statement case like *Ben-Shalom I* with the conduct features of *Hardwick,* to affix a characteristic of a *group* to one of its *members*.

Inducing the servicemember to make the factual concession that he has engaged in sodomy. When Steffan filed an equal protection challenge to his discharge in federal court, DOJ attorneys assigned to handle the defense took the next step. At a deposition arranged to investigate the factual support for Steffan's claim, they demanded that he tell them whether he had engaged in any homosexual acts. Steffan refused to answer; the government promptly moved to dismiss the case on grounds that he had violated every litigant's duty to answer all requests for relevant information; and the district court granted their motion (*Steffan A*). This strategy, if it had ultimately worked, would have absolved the government of the dirty work of imputing actual sodomy to Steffan as an individual by having him concede it.

The DOJ's new approach went beyond *Padula*'s *legal* claim that sodomy by a servicemember processed on the ground of his gay-identifying statement brought the case within the shadow of *Hardwick*, to make a *factual* assertion that this particular servicemember had engaged in sodomy. The government sought factual evidence of Steffan's conduct in the discovery process; if Steffan had responded by describing homosexual acts he had engaged in, the government would have moved to dismiss his case on the legal grounds that *Hardwick* foreclosed his claim. Conduct would then be the artifact not of legal attribution (as it appeared in the *Padula* formula and in Steffan's NIS report), but of factual investigation (*Steffan A* 124). If this strategy had worked, statement cases would have become conduct cases on their facts no later than discovery, and would have become so difficult to win that anti-gay discrimination in the military would have been secured from judicial examination.

For two reasons this strategy was not the home run government lawyers no doubt hoped it would be. First, the

D.C. Court of Appeals rejected the underlying legal rule and required the Army to defend Steffan's separation on the grounds actually invoked to achieve it (*Steffan B*). At least in the D.C. Circuit, statement cases could not become conduct cases in discovery. And second, the theory was not as elegant as it initially seemed. Even if it had prevailed, it could be asserted only when a servicemember sued, and thus well after his or her separation was complete. This was too late to alter the actual basis for separation. Steffan's silence was at worst a discovery violation; the original adverse action against him still rested on his identity statements.

For all its defects, however, the DOJ's new strategy had one signal advantage. If it had worked, the fact of Steffan's homosexual conduct would have entered the case in a new way. The strategy depended not on any positive evidence of sodomitical conduct obtained and held by the government, but on *Steffan's* failure to testify that *no such evidence existed.* Under this strategy, servicemembers would render their own lawsuits vulnerable to dismissal; by refusing to answer questions about their conduct, *they* would establish a conduct-related ground for *their own* loss of legal rights. Steffan's silence, while it did not establish any facts, at least involved him in generating the basis for some part of his own adversity.

In this respect the *Steffan* discovery demand is the formal predecessor of one of the most effective devices in the New DOD Policy. The rebuttable presumption of a propensity to commit homosexual acts, like the discovery demand, imputes the crucial factual concession to the servicemember. As anti-gay procedure, moreover, the rebuttable presumption device is a big improvement over the discovery demand, because, when deployed as part of separation proceedings, it eliminates the discovery demand's defect of operating after the fact.

We have in *Steffan*, then, the seeds of the 1993 revisions' procedures. The complete genesis of the rebuttable presumption device can't be understood, however, without an inquiry into the provenance of the propensity concept.

Imputing a propensity to commit sodomy as a matter of law. In *Ben-Shalom* and *Steffan*, Naval officials and DOJ lawyers struggled to make conduct not just a legal but a factual attribute of statement cases, not just a feature of the group of "homosexuals" but a deed of each individual in it. Their dilemma was to achieve this shift to factual, individual attribution without abandoning the advantages of group attribution as a matter of law. All the while, the language that DOJ lawyers would eventually promote as the solution to this dilemma lay unnoticed in a justificatory preamble to the Old DOD Policy. In a passage that DOJ lawyers only gradually realized could be mobilized to infuse a conduct meaning into statement cases, this preamble stated that "persons who engage in homosexual conduct or *who, by their statements, demonstrate a propensity to engage in homosexual conduct,* seriously impair[] the accomplishment of the military mission."

The link between the preamble's propensity clause and *Hardwick* seems to have been noticed first by Ninth Circuit Court of Appeals Judge Reinhardt, in his dissent from a three-judge decision holding that the Army had violated the equal protection clause when it denied reenlistment to Sergeant Perry Watkins because he had said he was gay (*Watkins B*). From his enlistment in 1967 until his security clearance was revoked in 1980, Watkins

79

had repeatedly told Army officials that he was gay, and was persistently reenlisted, granted security clearances, and promoted nevertheless (*Watkins A* 215–17; *Watkins B* 1331–33). Trial and appellate courts disagreed with pendulum regularity about whether they needed to reach Watkins's claim that the equal protection clause was violated in his case or whether they could rule instead on a ground that might well have been unique to Watkins's case, his estoppel claim that the Army could not object to his homosexual identity after having accepted it for so long. The panel decision in *Watkins B* gave Watkins a favorable constitutional ruling, but it was later vacated by the Ninth Circuit acting *en banc,* which ultimately held for Watkins on estoppel grounds (*Watkins C*).[5]

Dissenting in 1988 from *Watkins B,* Judge Reinhardt insisted that *Hardwick* foreclosed Watkins's equal-protection claim because the propensity preamble guided interpretation of the entire policy: "*Read in this light,* the regulations constitute an attempt to exclude those who engage in or will engage in homosexual acts. . . . In my opinion, the regulations are targeted at conduct—past, present and future, but conduct nonetheless" (*Watkins B* 1361–62; emphasis added). Judge Reinhardt construed the Old DOD Policy's preamble to provide a legal definition of the social group regulators sought to exclude, and to do it well enough to provide the basis for judicial deference to any imprecisions it might present. The regulations are an *attempt* to target conduct, and to identify those *most likely* to have engaged, to engage, or to be about to engage in it. Like the *Padula* court's announcement that sodomy is the behavior that defines the class of homosexuals, Judge Reinhardt's logic gives *legal* rather than *factual* definition to a *group* rather than an *individual*. From the perspective of DOJ lawyers it must have appeared a vast improvement over the *Padula* formula, moreover, because it mobilized part of the very policy they were defending.

The full advantages of Judge Reinhardt's suggestion became clear only a year later, in the Seventh Circuit's decision in *Ben-Shalom II*. Miriam Ben-Shalom's second lawsuit originated in her first one. After she won her 1980 judgment requiring the Army to reinstate her, the Army refused to comply over the course of eleven long years of legal wrangling that did not (to the government's perpetual shame) include an appeal on the merits (*Ben-Shalom II A* 1373–74). When it finally obeyed the trial court's order, Ben-Shalom's enlistment was about to expire, giving the Army the opportunity to deny her reenlistment. Hence *Ben-Shalom II*.

In *Ben-Shalom II* the Seventh Circuit restated the propensity concept in a way that encompassed both its actuarial and psychometric meanings. Sodomy emerges both as the probable, predicted, risked behavior of people who say they are gay and as their own certain and particularized past deed. It was as though the court had placed the group/individual and law/fact dichotomies in suspension.

The factual record hadn't changed: the Army denied Ben-Shalom reenlistment for the same statements that had provided the grounds for her initial separation. But the regulations had changed quite a bit: whereas *Ben-Shalom I* tested Army regulations requiring the separation of any servicemember who "evidences homosexual tendencies, desire, or interest, but is without overt homosexual acts" (Army Reg. 135–178, ch. 7–5b(6)), *Ben-*

Shalom II involved the Old DOD Policy, which provided for the separation of any servicemember who has "stated that he or she is a homosexual or bisexual unless there is a further finding that the member is not a homosexual or bisexual" and which included the preamble justification that military effectiveness is impaired by servicemembers who, "by their statements, demonstrate a propensity to engage in homosexual conduct." The trial court in *Ben-Shalom II* determined that the shift to the Old DOD Policy was a distinction without a difference: if the Army violated the Constitution by excluding Ben-Shalom because her statements evidenced homosexual tendencies, it violated the Constitution again by excluding her because her statements established that she was a homosexual; both actions were based on her status, and her speech about it, and violated the equal-protection and free-speech clauses (*Ben-Shalom II A*). The Seventh Circuit reversed, and held for the Army, on the ground that the Army's second effort to get rid of Ben-Shalom was based on conduct of which it had no evidence. The propensity rationale was the hinge upon which this reversal turned.

"Propensity" in the Seventh Circuit's decision bestows the advantages of the actuarial model of propensity on a frankly psychometric use of the term. Invoking an actuarial conception of propensity-based anti-gay regulation, the Seventh Circuit established that the military is properly a risk-averse organization: "[W]e do not believe that the Army has to assume the risk that the presence of homosexuals within the service will not compromise the admittedly significant government interests" at stake (*Ben-Shalom II B* 460). In fact, the Army is so risk averse that it should not be required even to have a very clear idea of how homosexuals might affect it: "[T]he Army should not be required by this court to assume the risk . . . that accepting admitted homosexuals into the armed forces might imperil morale, discipline, and the effectiveness of our fighting forces" (*Ben-Shalom II B* 461). If the Army has decided that homosexuals on average are more likely than others to engage in harmful conduct, the court held, it can exclude all of them without needing to take fairness to individuals into account: "The Army need not try to fine tune a regulation to fit a particular lesbian's subjective thoughts and propensities" (*Ben-Shalom II B* 464). The idea that a "*particular lesbian*" has "*subjective . . . propensities,*" however, presupposes that propensities are inner character traits ("tendencies"?) that direct her to predictable behavior.

In some passages of the opinion this implicit divergence from the actuarial model is not terribly pronounced. For instance, the court admitted that, while the Old DOD Policy focused on conduct by the particular soldier, it dealt with the *risk* rather than the *certainty* of such conduct: "the Army does not have to take the risk that an admitted homosexual will not commit homosexual acts which may be detrimental to its assigned mission" (*Ben-Shalom II B* 460–61). Similarly, it determined that a servicemember's statement of his or her homosexual identity was enough to establish the presence of such a risk: "acknowledgement of being a lesbian without proof of actual homosexual conduct equals *reliable evidence of 'propensity'*" (*Ben-Shalom II B* 459; emphasis added).

But elsewhere the court demonstrated virtually absolute certainty that anyone with a propensity to commit an act must inevitably, ineluctably actually commit it—indeed that Ben-Shalom not only *might commit* or *might have committed* but *had committed* criminal sodomy. Inviting the court to make a gesture akin to the NIS finding that Joseph Steffan had violated the UCMJ sodomy statute, the government argued that Ben-Shalom's identity statements were admissions that *she personally* was "likely to engage in *criminal acts of sodomy*" and that this likelihood needed no proof because it was an "obvious connection" readily apparent to "common sense" (*Ben-Shalom II A* 1375, 1377; emphasis added). Though the trial court had

rejected this logic, the Seventh Circuit embraced it and proceeded one step further. It reasoned: "Plaintiff's lesbian acknowledgment, if not an admission of its practice, at least can rationally and reasonably be viewed as reliable evidence of a desire and propensity to engage in homosexual conduct. Such an assumption cannot be said to be without individual exceptions, but it is compelling evidence that *plaintiff has in the past and is likely to again* engage in such conduct. . . . To this extent, therefore, the regulation does not classify plaintiff based merely upon her status as a lesbian, but upon reasonable inferences about *her probable conduct in the past and in the future*" (*Ben-Shalom II B* 464; emphases added).

The inferential process here is this. First, it was reasonable for the Army to infer, from Ben-Shalom's statement that she was a lesbian, that she desired to engage in homosexual acts and had a propensity to engage in them. Second, it was reasonable for the Army to infer from her propensity to engage in homosexual acts that she probably had engaged or would soon engage in them. And third, the propensity inference is "*compelling evi-*

dence" that she "*has . . . engage[d]*" in them. There is the daring but subtle move from group to individual attribution, from legal definition to fact finding, from the actuarial to the psychometric model of propensity. If the court could say that, then there was nothing to hinder its next move: *Hardwick* applies to bar strict equal-protection scrutiny of this statement-based case because "*her conduct*, at the very least, *has an impact* upon other soldiers" (*Ben-Shalom II B* 465; emphasis added). You couldn't write that sentence unless you thought either that the possibility of conduct was conclusive proof of its actuality, or that possibility and actuality were not different concepts. And you couldn't hold either of those positions unless you thought that status defined conduct.

In the Seventh Circuit's decision in *Ben-Shalom II*, "propensity" mediates between actuarial and psychometric apprehensions of Miriam Ben-Shalom, keeping them both available as rhetorical resources. The resulting rhetorical range is remarkable: apologetics for military anti-gay policy could, and did, toggle at will from nominalist, empirically skeptical, and anormative justifications to realist, empirically confident, and morally judgmental ones, and back again. The DOJ went on to insist that propensity should accrue the probative advantages both of its actuarial and of its psychometric forms. Propensity thus entered into the prolegomenon to the 1993 debates with all the systematic fluidity of the status/conduct distinction as it was deployed by the *Hardwick* majority. What it lacked was a procedural form capable of masking this lexical volatility.

Inducing the servicemember to make a factual concession that he himself has a propensity to engage in homosexual conduct. The problem with the reworking of the propensity concept in *Ben-Shalom II* is its obvious legerdemain, its lack of justification for attributing *this type of conduct* to *this servicemember.* The solution was the famous, and widely misunderstood, "rebuttable presumption of a propensity." Attorney General Janet Reno and Clinton administration officials lauded this change for giving servicemembers an "opportunity to rebut" (wн4; Reno Memo).

This description of the rebuttable presumption was particularly disingenuous. Presumptions are burden-shifting devices, a procedural means of setting the default loser just as a word-processing program sets a default margin (James, Hazard, and Leubsdorf § 7.12). But being a default loser is a lot more unpleasant than being a default margin. It would have been more honest and more consistent with legal usage if defenders of the 1993 revisions had said they were making servicemembers *bear the burden* of rebutting the presumption.

Presumptions are possibly the single easiest way to make sure that one party to a dispute steps up to the starting line with a heavy handicap. They are a classic way to achieve substantive outcomes under the guise of a merely technical change in procedure. As if that weren't enough, the rebuttable presumption of a propensity offered an array of legal and rhetorical advantages to proponents of military anti-gay policy. Most decisively, proponents of the 1993 revisions claim that giving a servicemember an "opportunity" to rebut a presumption that he or she has a propensity to engage in homosexual conduct transforms a legal and actuarial prediction about a group into a *fact* about *that servicemember.* This procedural "improvement" purports to put conduct *into this case, at the time of separation.*

More rhetorically, the Clinton administration's political appeals on behalf of the 1993 revisions emphasized that the rebuttable-presumption device extracts a concession from a servicemember being processed for discharge that she, personally, cannot or will not "play by the rules" of military society. An "opportunity to rebut" was fair, they insisted, because it gave servicemembers the last best chance to avoid the train wreck of separation, and thus the blame for not taking advantage of it.

Proponents of the 1993 revisions praised the rebuttal burden for shifting regulatory attention from status to conduct, and thus advancing beyond the bad old days of status regulation under the Old DOD Policy. At the same time, when Aspin announced the New DOD Policy, he insisted that the "rebuttable presumption" it introduced was merely carried over from the Old DOD Policy (Cong.2 39, 26). So which version is right? In a sense both are: the rebuttable presumption device translates the Old DOD Policy into new terms that preserve, while hiding, its focus on status. Just as maintaining the propensity concept in its actuarial and psychometric meanings gave apologists for anti-gay policy access to contradictory, though complementary, models of their project and thus great rhetorical flexibility, so the representation of the presumption device as novel-but-the-same seeks to propitiate public appetites for progressive change and for conservative rigor. More fundamentally, it locates the putative change in a lexical rather than real operation of the propensity device. And more fundamentally still, it indicates that, in the new representational system set up by the 1993 revision, "status" does not disappear but rather recedes into the background, where it functions as the purportedly excluded term whose presence, though suppressed, is crucial to the meaning of "conduct."

The Old DOD Policy did not ask servicemembers being processed for discharge to prove anything about their past or future conduct. Instead, it offered them two status-based defenses: it required the discharge of any "member [who] has stated that he or she is *a homosexual or bisexual* unless there is a further finding that the member is not *a homosexual or bisexual*"; and it required discharge of anyone who had engaged in "homosexual acts" unless he or she could satisfy the four-step queen-for-a-day test. Before the propensity concept entered circulation, courts construing the Old DOD Policy were clear that its defenses focused on status, even as they began to introduce the idea that the policy created a "rebuttable presumption." Miriam Ben-Shalom's commanding officer, for instance, "advised [her] . . . that her admission of homosexuality gave rise to a *presumption that she was a homosexual,* and that she therefore [must] submit a response rebutting that presumption" (*Ben-Shalom II B* 457; emphasis added).[6] And Judge Canby wrote in his panel decision in *Watkins B* (the one that provoked Judge Reinhardt's important dissent) that the queen-for-a-day provisions of the Old DOD Policy "clearly mandate that homosexual acts give rise to a disqualifying presumption of homosexuality, though that presumption can be rebutted by proof of actual nonhomosexual orientation" (*Watkins B* 1335; emphasis added). These are, quite explicitly, status defenses.

Ensuing iterations of the Old DOD Policy's status de-

88

fenses translated them, step by step, into a rebuttable presumption of a propensity. The most important changes were made in DOJ's reading of the rules applied to separations based on statements. The DOJ made two key moves in these cases. First, it insisted that the Old DOD Policy's requirement that the servicemember prove that she "was not a homosexual or bisexual" turned on the policy's definition of "homosexual" as "a person . . . who engages in, desires to engage in, or intends to engage in homosexual acts." And second, it transmuted that three-part definition into a bar not on homosexuals but on persons with a propensity to engage in homosexual acts.

The *Steffan* litigation was a laboratory for this translation. The government took the first step I have been able to identify in 1990, when it submitted a brief to the D.C. Circuit in the *Steffan* discovery dispute. In this submission, which I will call the Government's 1990 Brief, DOJ lawyers insisted that "although Steffan was separated based on his *admission* of homosexuality, he was *not* separated based solely on his homosexual orientation. Rather, his admission of homosexuality gave rise to a *rebuttable regulatory presumption of homosexual proclivity and conduct, which Steffan refused to rebut in 1987 and which he still refuses to rebut*" (CP9 15–16; third emphasis added). Here the DOJ restated the Old DOD Policy's status exception ("if there is a further finding that the servicemember is not a homosexual") as a "proclivity and conduct" rebuttal. It is pretty clear, however, that DOJ lawyers were not yet asking the court to follow Judge Reinhardt in "[r]ead[ing the grounds for discharge] in light of" the Old DOD Policy's introductory term "propensity." "Proclivity" appears in the brief eight times for every instance of the term "propensity," a clear indication that the DOJ did not yet realize how useful the preamble language would prove to be. It is even clearer that they then understood a proclivity to be a psychometric inner disposition of persons, not an actuarial behavioral observation about a class. The Government's 1990 Brief persistently presents the term "proclivity" as a shorthand substitute for the "desires . . . or intends" terms of the Old DOD Policy's definition of "homosexual" (CP9 19–21), and at one point compares a servicemember deemed to have a "proclivity" to engage in homosexual conduct to "a servicemember who publicly admitted that he was an arsonist or a kleptomaniac" (CP9 34). The term "proclivity" retains all the personhood assumptions of the Old DOD Policy's status defenses.

The introduction of "proclivity" nevertheless indicates the DOJ's willingness to defend military anti-gay policy by redescribing it—a willingness that is even more remarkable in the DOJ's insistence that the Old DOD Policy introduced the rebuttable-presumption device, and had done so in Steffan's case. In the Government's 1990 Brief, DOJ lawyers claimed that Steffan had had an opportunity to rebut the presumption in 1987, when he was originally processed for discharge—though we know that, at that time, Navy officials were content to conclude that Steffan had engaged in criminal sodomy on the sole grounds of his statement that he was gay. That brief also implicitly asserted that the trial court had granted the discovery dismissal on the ground of Steffan's failure to shoulder a burden of rebutting conduct—an argument which the Court of Appeals could not detect in the government's submissions to the trial court (nor, I would add, can I), and which it accordingly treated as waived (*Steffan B* 76 n.).

Several years later in the *Steffan* litigation the DOJ went on to upgrade the "proclivity" concept as well. The stimulus may have been a canny footnote in Judge Reinhardt's dissent in Watkins, in which he warned that a gay plaintiff who complained that the Old DOD Policy discriminated against him on the basis of status-not-conduct would be logically compelled to say his injury would be remedied if a court struck the "desires" element from the regulations' definition of "homosexual," allowing the miliary to reprocess him for discharge under the language that remained (*Watkins B* 1460 n. 22). Steffan's lawyers mobilized this concession that discrimination on the basis of desires might be unconstitutional status discrimination by emphasizing the way in which the Old DOD Policy excluded servicemembers on the basis of "who they are"; of "one aspect of their personality"; of "personal inclinations"; and of "a person's thoughts" (CP10 8, 9, 30). "Proclivities" as desires were indeed vulnerable to constitutional objection at that time. In an important, though ephemeral, victory for Steffan, a panel of the D.C. Circuit had held in November 1993 that the Old DOD Policy was unconstitutional because its regulation of "the content of [Steffan's] thoughts . . . is repugnant to the various common law and constitutional principles that guard the sanctity of a person's thoughts against government control" (*Steffan D* 76). "Thoughts and desires" were consistently linked in the opinion, locating the constitutional weak spot in the Old DOD Policy in its regulation of desires (*Steffan D* 64, 66). Though in January 1994 the

D.C. Circuit acting *en banc* vacated the panel decision in
Steffan, and in May 1994 the *en banc* court issued a decision repudiating the panel decision's rationale (*Steffan
E*), throughout 1993 the DOJ had good reason to take the
attack on "desires" seriously. If proclivities were nothing
but desires, their regulation was in some constitutional
jeopardy (so they had to be something else).

The DOJ addressed the "desires" crisis in *Steffan* in two
important briefs: a 1993 brief submitted to the panel of
the D.C. Circuit that ultimately ruled for Steffan, and a
1994 brief submitted to the *en banc* court that later issued
a formal decision in favor of the government. I will designate these submissions the Government's 1993 Brief and
the Government's 1994 Brief, respectively. The Government's 1993 Brief jettisoned the term "proclivity," thus
dissociating itself from the sneering psychometric signification which that term (like "tendencies") has had in
anti-gay culture. In its place appears the formerly un-
appreciated term "propensity": "the regulatory definition of 'homosexual' is linked to homosexual *acts and the
propensity* to commit homosexual acts" (CP11 21). And indeed, all the DOJ seems to have wanted was a "link": the
brief did what it could to muddle the relationship of propensity to desire, alternatively positing "propensity" as
the equivalent of desire (CP11 16, 38), the equivalent of intent (CP11 4, 22), and the equivalent of homosexual desire
and intent (CP11 21, 26 n. 9, 41) and ultimately using it as
a recapitulation of the regulation *tout court.*

It was not easy to do away with the psychometric concept of propensity, however. Facing up to the need for
a definition of "desires," the Government's 1993 Brief
equivocated about whether they are sustained intentions

to act or character traits: "The meaning that DoD attributes to the regulatory term 'desire' is informed by its context and by the term 'propensity.' Pursuant to DoD's interpretation, a service member's expressed 'desire' to commit homosexual acts evidences more than an abstract, ephemeral, or suppressible whim. *Like acts themselves and like intentions,* 'desire' in the relevant sense evidences a 'propensity,' or an *'often intense natural inclination,'* *Webster's New Collegiate Dictionary* 943 (9th ed. 1990), to commit serious regulatory violations" (CP11 21 n. 7; emphasis added).

Rebuked by the D.C. Circuit's panel decision holding **93** that the Old DOD Policy unconstitutionally monitored Steffan's thoughts, DOJ lawyers rewrote this passage in the Government's 1994 Brief, redefining "desires" to implicate acts and intentions *and not* personhood: "Whatever ambiguity this word may have in isolation, DoD interprets it as conduct-directed in light of both the overarching standard of 'propensity,' Directive 1331.14.H.I, and the surrounding terms 'engages in' and 'intends to engage in' homosexual acts. *Id.* H.1.b(l). Moreover, this interpretation is consistent with accepted definitions of the term desires. *See, e.g., Black's Law Dictionary* 448 (6th ed. 1990) ('desire' defined as '[t]o ask, to request' and cross-referencing 'intent'); *The Random House Dictionary of the English Language* 539 (1987) ('desire' defined as 'to express a wish to obtain; ask for; request')" (CP12 19–20). The usage invoked here is archaic, certainly: since when do Americans asking a favor say, "I desire you to give me that letter"? The tension in this redefinition indicates a late realization that it was bad anti-gay strategy to describe desires as an attribute of persons, and suggests that by 1993 the DOJ had finally gotten a steady grasp on the rhetorical advantages of the actuarial model of propensity.

These are most prominently on display wherever the Government's 1993 Brief states the governmental purposes of the Old DOD Policy, a task it achieves without adopting the term "homosexual." The court was urged to suppose that military leaders weren't worried about a type of person but about the likelihood of harmful conduct. Their mission was so urgent and difficult (CP11 37) that they should not have to take the risk of such conduct (CP11 38). The brief systematically takes up the non-normative posture made possible by the actuarial model: anti-gay troops weren't homophobic, they were just "disturb[ed]" by the possibility of misconduct (CP11 40) and military top brass's decision to respond to troop opinion, far from endorsing a normative judgment, was mere sound management (CP11 39). And if the military in its prudent vigilance happened to exclude some men or women who would never violate its standards of conduct—hey, every actuarial group includes members who will not experience the casualty insured against, but it still is rational to pool the risk and charge them a pro rata share of its cost (CP11 43).

The actuarial model thus provides the legal justification for the Old DOD Policy, and seems to supplant the psychometric model of propensity altogether. Yet again, however, not so. The textual revisionism of the DOJ's late *Steffan* briefs suppresses, while retaining, the psychometric model of propensity: by implicitly insisting on the unimpeded translatability of status into conduct terms, they simultaneously abandon and retain status concepts. At its simplest this practice produces episodes, like the *re*-retranslation of "desires," in which psychometric uses of propensity subside so as to yield prominence to actuarial ones. That the DOJ never pretended this shift was anything but a lexical substitution is indicated by a frankly palimpsestic quotation in the Government's 1993 Brief: the brief substituted "propensity" for the district court's term "preferences," marking its handiwork with brackets![7]

The boldest textual revision offered in the late *Steffan* briefs is also the one in which status concepts are most crucial and most hidden. Although DOJ lawyers could not afford to invoke the psychometric model of propensity during the "desires" crisis, they simultaneously, and nevertheless, needed it to make sense of their keystone procedural argument, that a *rebuttable presumption of a propensity* cleansed the Old DOD Policy of its focus on status.

This point will be clearer if we look ahead for a moment. The argument that the rebuttable presumption of a propensity makes Aspin's New DOD Policy acts-based *and not* status-based depends on the power of that procedural device to attribute to an individual servicemember being processed for discharge the factual concession that he has engaged in prohibited conduct. Let's suppose the rebuttable-presumption device had been in place under the Old DOD Policy. If a servicemember refused to contest the presumption, or offered rebuttal evidence that failed to convince the hearing board that he or she lacked a propensity, the board would have been legally constrained to conclude that the presumption had not been defeated. The formal operation of the rebuttable-presumption device would then convert the presumption into a factual "finding"—a legal fact as "real," for purposes of these proceedings, as any finding supported by positive record evidence. The rebuttable-presumption device would have eliminated any need to refer to the personal character of the servicemember, to suppose him or her to have psychological proclivities/preferences/tendencies/desires, or to do anything that would in any way invoke the psychometric model of propensity. At the same time, it would have eliminated any need to produce evidence of sexual conduct within the meaning of the regulations. Conduct would have come into the case *without evidence* but *as a fact,* because of the servicemember's own inability to disprove an imputed propensity to engage in it.

The problem with justifying Steffan's discharge on these grounds, of course, is that he was separated without being invited to rebut a presumption of a propensity. Navy officials' failure to proffer such a procedural opportunity is easy to explain: they hadn't thought it up yet! It would not be until six years later that DOJ lawyers would craft the rebuttable presumption of a propensity and make it the keystone of their defense of the policy. Now, treating the Old DOD Policy's procedures *as if they included* the rebuttable-presumption device requires a factual basis outside the device itself. After all, the rebuttable-presumption device serves to introduce conduct as a *fact,* but if it was not actually used it is no improvement whatsoever over the DOJ's earlier legal approaches. *The logical gap here could be filled only by a suppressed assumption that Steffan was irretrievably committed to sodomy by a natural bent of personality.* The psychometric model of propensity is a necessary moving part of the *Steffan* case as the government finally presented it:

though the briefs suppress it, it is merely hidden in plain sight.

Although the DOJ's new deployment of the actuarial model of propensity thus covertly depends on the psychometric model of propensity (and thus incorporates "status" as a premise in its logic for attributing "conduct"), the two models are also engaged in an important contradiction. Aside from bringing *Hardwick* to bear on statement cases, the great legal achievement of the actuarial model of propensity is its jigsaw fit to rational-basis review. As the DOJ reminded the D.C. Circuit panel, " '[d]ischarge of [a given individual] would be rational, under minimal scrutiny, not because [his] particular case[] present[s] the dangers which justify Navy policy, but instead because the general policy is rational" (CP11 43, quoting *Beller* 808–9 n. 20). Overbroad application of the classification to individual servicemembers without evidence of conduct is precisely what this rational-basis argument excuses.

Thus the government says it does *not* intend to allow individual servicemembers to prove themselves out of the classification; but that is precisely what the rebuttable-presumption device purports to make possible. Steffan's case is a paradigm example, moreover, of how the rebuttable presumption of a propensity can be deployed as a legal fiction, stripped of any referential content whatsoever, and converted into an *ir*rebuttable presumption that introduces conduct into status cases by legal fiat. Steffan's having an opportunity to rebut and his not having such an opportunity were, to DOJ lawyers redescribing the Old DOD Policy, transparent translations of one another.

The factual foundation of Steffan's separation *appears* to be conduct but *really (covertly) was* his answer to the question, "Are you a homosexual?": "Yes, sir, I am." Yet once more, a status ascription provides the hidden foundation for the propensity concept's acts-based rationales. And an even more distasteful exploitation of contradictory premises has been revealed here: the so-called opportunity to rebut can be deployed as a bald ruse, in which the servicemember is purported to be treated as an agent responsible for his own misfortune, but is actually the scrim upon which the status/conduct distinction, in all its shimmering volatility, is played.

From the propensity concept to the 1993 revisions. The DOJ submitted the Government's 1993 Brief on July 29 — ten days after the Clinton administration announced the New DOD Policy. The relationship between them is both direct and complex. The 1993 policy revisions gave DOJ attorneys an opportunity to write new regulations and ultimately legislation that fixed what they thought was broken in the Old DOD Policy.[8] The fact that, at the same time, the procedural wrangling in *Steffan* ended propelling the litigation to the question of whether or not the Old DOD Policy was constitutional, gave them an opportunity to obtain early judicial approval for the New DOD Policy by litigating the old one under its description.[9] That these efforts present a contradiction should not surprise anyone. And the importance of players whose job was justifying the Old DOD Policy, not reforming it, should remind us that the 1993 revisions, far from making military policy less anti-gay or less status-based, merely made it more subtly so.

Enforcement

Having claimed that the rebuttable-presumption device is rational because it institutes an actuarial practice that results, by necessity, in overbroad application, the Department of Justice implicitly conceded that the "opportunity" to rebut may be nothing but a formality. But "may be" is not the same as "is": in order to understand the rebuttable-presumption device, we need to know how military enforcers actually do deploy the systematic mutabilities of the status/conduct distinction.

A key index of enforcement is the phase of individual servicemembers' board hearings when they are required to rebut the presumption of a propensity: how do they respond, and how do hearing boards react? Defending various cases when the 1993 revisions were brand new, the DOJ submitted a set of seven hearing transcripts in which, the DOJ claimed, the presumption was successfully rebutted. These "Seven Exhibits," [10] taken together with hearing transcripts not included in the DOJ submissions which I have obtained by other means, provide the basis for some predictions about how the DOJ will ask courts to interpret the propensity clauses.

The courts that have considered the Seven Exhibits have disagreed about whether they show that the presumption cannot be rebutted by evidence short of a recantation of homosexual identity (*Holmes A* 1528–29; *Able C* 976; see also *Holmes B* 1140 [Reinhardt, J., dissenting]), or that it can (*Richenberg A* 1313–17; *Richenberg C* 262; *Thomasson B* 932; *Thorne* B 927–29; *Able D* 1297–98; *Holmes B* 1135). And no wonder: the infusion of status concepts into the language of conduct, and the persistent volatility of the resulting lexical system, make rebuttal cases intrinsically unpredictable. But some patterns do emerge. Strikingly, each distinct type of case — "the Heterosexually Loyal Bisexual," "Deny Acts," "Eagle Scout," and "Rewrite the Statute" — contributes to a single conclusion: that the presumption can be rebutted only by affirmations of heterosexual status. Not only that: taken together they reveal a DOJ willing to lead some federal judges to suppose that the presumption is rebuttable by evidence that it tells other judges is irrelevant.

The strongest rebuttal case apparent on this record is that of the "Heterosexually Loyal Bisexual." In this category are two male servicemembers who testified that they were bisexual and provided some other evidence showing that they would opt to find sexual release not with men but with women (Seven Exhibits No. 3 and No. 6). In Seven Exhibits No. 3 the servicemember repeated that he was a "homosexual"; gave what he admitted was "confused" testimony that he had "feelings toward men and women" but "sexual feelings" and "desires" only for women; and stated that he had decided not to engage in same-sex conduct because of his fear of "catching a disease." In Seven Exhibits No. 6, both the servicemember and his wife testified about their marital loyalty, the quality of their sexual relationship (excellent), and the way in which the servicemember's disclosure of his bisexuality had actually strengthened their marriage.

One would have thought that the proof in Seven Exhibits No. 6 went almost over the top, but even in that case one of three board members voted that the servicemember had not rebutted the presumption. Nevertheless, this seems to be the only relatively secure strategy so far: I have no evidence that any hearing board has rejected such evidence, or that the DOJ has ever told anyone that it is legally insufficient. The DOJ tolerates the "Heterosexually Loyal Bisexual" not because the servicemember has done anything to disprove his propensity to homosexual acts, but because he has demonstrated an ability to adhere to heterosexual status.

The Seven Exhibits exemplify three weaker strategies, the legal adequacy of which must remain in some doubt. Though the DOJ argued when it submitted these Exhibits to federal trial judges that the success of these strategies shows that the presumption of a propensity is rebuttable, *it also has argued elsewhere that at least two of them are legally insufficient to rebut the presumption.* These three equivocal avenues can be dubbed "Deny Acts," "Eagle Scout," and "Rewrite the Statute."

To "Deny Acts," a servicemember has to deny homosexual acts, past and/or future, and/or the desire or intention to engage in them. Two servicemembers, apparently, have successfully rebutted the presumption in this way. In Seven Exhibits No. 2, the servicemember testified merely that she intended to obey "all rules and regulations prohibiting homosexual conduct" (355); a bevy of witnesses testified to her general good character and good work habits but none of them was able to corroborate her lack of a propensity; and the board was nevertheless satisfied (401). In Seven Exhibits No. 5, the servicemember's attorney stated that his client had not engaged in homosexual acts while in the Air Force, or, in one iteration, while on active duty; the servicemember indicated that his religious faith would enable him to avoid homosexual conduct, and put his chaplain on the stand to corroborate him on this point; and on this slightly stronger record the board was, again, satisfied that the presumption had been rebutted (Chapman Declaration 7–8).

The "Deny Acts" strategy has failed, however, on much stronger evidence than that offered in Seven Exhibits No. 2 and No. 5. Air Force Captain Richard F. Richenberg testified that he had only recently realized that he was homosexual; that his statement that he was homosexual described only his "orientation" and not his conduct; and that he had not engaged in, and did not intend to engage in, prohibited conduct (Richenberg Trans. 149). He made a clear distinction between homosexual "attraction" and "doing it"; stated that even if he were not in the military he would be governed by his moral disapproval of "casual sex"; and corroborated this statement by testimony that, when he still understood himself to be heterosexual, he had had close relationships with women but had honored his belief that sexual intercourse should await marriage (Richenberg Trans. 147, 156).

Richenberg's fate throws doubt on the DOJ's claim that "Deny Acts" is a viable rebuttal strategy for two reasons. First, his board held that he had not rebutted the presumption (Richenbert Trans. 184). Second, the DOJ insisted, and convinced the trial court in Richenberg's case, that "It is of no constitutional significance that the plaintiff may in fact have no propensity to engage in homosexual conduct" (*Richenberg A* 12). This emergence of the actuarial model of a propensity flatly contradicts the DOJ's resort to the psychometric model every time it seeks to persuade a federal court that the rebuttable presumption effectively selects some servicemembers for retention because *they* lack a propensity.

"Eagle Scout" evidence is proof of the servicemember's excellent reputation and general loyalty to military values. Most servicemembers being processed for discharge under the Statute present this species of evidence; few rely on it to the exclusion of all testimony about their sexual conduct. And for good reason: "Deny Acts," which is at least relevant to the presumption, is nevertheless unreliable; "Eagle Scout" when presented alone is likely to be seen as simply nonresponsive (*Selland II* 263). The servicemember in Seven Exhibits No. 7 took the risk, and won.

Inasmuch as "Eagle Scout" evidence is logically inapposite to the rebuttal burden actually placed on the servicemember's shoulders, the DOJ's attempt to prove to the federal trial courts that the presumption is rebuttable by pointing to its success in Exhibit No. 7 amounts to an acknowledgment of the vast extralegal discretion allowed to hearing boards under the Statute. Seven Exhibits No. 1 shows that this discretion may reduce to nothing more than the hearing board's power to decide how homophobic to be. In that case the servicemember had two boards: the first heard witnesses, while the second ruled on the basis of the record produced by the first hearing. In the first hearing the servicemember denied an intention to engage in acts, and relied primarily on a parade of "Eagle Scout" witnesses from his division. In response, the recorder (the military equivalent of a prosecutor) provided no evidence of conduct, and instead collected several witnesses at the last minute who did not know the servicemember and who testified only to their own anti-gay attitudes. The first board recommended separation; the second board, acting on a virtually identical record, recommended retention (Chapman Declaration 3–4). These divergent results display the range of discretion granted by the 1993 revisions to military decision-makers. The propensity term is so malleable that the outcome reached by a particular board indicates nothing more than its homophobic, homo-neutral, or homophilic propensities.

Most astonishing of all the Seven Exhibits, however, is No. 4. Though it is stripped of all identifying names in court papers, it matches page for page the transcript of Navy Reserve Lieutenant Maria Zoe Dunning. Dunning offered to rebut the presumption by testifying that her statement that she is a lesbian merely described "who I am"—her "orientation"—and was "in no way meant to imply any propensity or intent or desire to engage in prohibited conduct" (Dunning Trans. 233)—and she won (289). Her testimony may be even more nonresponsive than "Eagle Scout" evidence: at least the latter, when coupled with a denial of an intent, offers to bolster the servicemember's credibility. Dunning, with subtle boldness, denied not an intent to engage in homosexual acts but an intent to raise a presumption of a propensity! I've dubbed this the "Rewrite the Statute" strategy; as far as I know, Dunning is the only servicemember still in uniform after adopting it.

When the DOJ lawyers produced the Dunning transcript as evidence that the presumption of a propensity could be rebutted, they plunged into their most trenchant demonstration of the volatility of the Statute, and of its propensity terms, in actual enforcement. This is so not only because military lawyers at Dunning's hearing vigorously objected that her rebuttal was legally insufficient, and not only because in other cases DOJ lawyers, by submitting the Dunning transcript as one of the Seven Exhibits, endorsed Dunning's denial as a rebuttal, but also because DOJ lawyers so remarkably failed to direct any court's attention to a then-existing internal DOD memorandum warning commanders in all branches that the Dunning rebuttal is legally ineffective (DOD9 2).

Clearly the DOJ is energetically playing both sides of the street. It defends the constitutionality of the Statute because the presumption both is and is not rebuttable; it invokes the actuarial and psychometric models of a propensity in a way that accentuates their mutual contradiction; it claims that the Statute does not discriminate against homosexuals when the only secure rebuttal yet on record belongs to the "Heterosexually Loyal Bisexual"; it claims that servicemembers who state that they are gay can rebut by "Denying Acts" but then denies that such denials can rebut a propensity; it denies, then affirms, then denies that a servicemember can control the meaning of her coming-out statement.

In doing so the DOJ, and with it the DOD and military enforcers "on the ground," are taking advantage of a key, though silent, term of the 1993 pact between Congress, the White House, and military top brass: military discretion. When Aspin presented the New DOD Policy to Congress in the summer of 1993, a dispute broke out between Congress and military leaders about how much discretion should be afforded to line officers in enforcing the policy. The conflict emerged when Chairman of the Joint Chiefs General Colin Powell and all five Joint Chiefs toured the Senate and House Armed Services Committees at Aspin's side, making elaborate statements endorsing Aspin's proposal (DOD5; Schmitt, "Military Praises"). At this time Nunn was giving only conditional approval to the New

DOD Policy (Cong.5; Devroy, Schmitt, "In Break"); he and other members of Congress objected strongly at first to its lack of particularity. Nunn declared: "This has to be pinned down. We can't have a commander out there saying, 'What do I do,' and somebody says, 'Call the attorney general'" (Cong.2 35; Lancaster, "Senators Find"). Representative Cliff Stearns asserted that the policy's failure to provide strict anti-gay rules would merely provoke "quote, 'the traditional mischief' that starts in litigation" (Cong.3 49); while Representative Duncan Hunter warned about the policy's ambiguities: "It's going to be paradise for lawyers. . . . It's going to be a nightmare for our military people" (Cong.3 54).

The unequivocal support of the Joint Chiefs is striking by contrast. Whether they actually liked or merely accepted the New DOD Policy, it is clear that they didn't want Congress to draft a more directive statute. They responded with rising annoyance to every congressional suggestion that the New DOD Policy was defective because ambiguous or insufficiently rule-like. Powell warned the House Armed Services Committee: "This isn't a cookie-cutter solution that can be applied from Washington." When Senator John McCain objected that "This [policy] places an incredible burden on commanders in the field," Army Major General John P. Otjen rebuked him: "Our commanding officers are making these kind [*sic*] of decisions all the time right now" (Schmitt, "Military Praises"). The Joint Chiefs got help from Secretary of Defense Aspin, who, faced with questions about how the New DOD Policy would apply in particular cases, curtly warned the senators off: "Under this policy, the commander is the arbiter of all gray area decisions"

(Lancaster, "Joint Chiefs"). Clearly the Clinton administration and the Joint Chiefs had reached an agreement that, to the extent that the New DOD Policy was ambiguous or interpretable, its elaboration should be delegated to the Department of Defense and the military branches. Nothing in the Statute interferes with this agreement.

The key ambiguity which military discretion manipulates is the range of meaning attributable to "homosexual conduct." The Statute defines this term as "bodily contact which a reasonable person would understand to demonstrate a propensity . . . to engage in" erotic, same-sex bodily contacts. This language is subject to some remarkable manipulations, along two distinct dimensions. First, as I describe in the next section, "contact" itself has been given an alarmingly unbounded construal. And second, as I describe in the following section, indexing conduct that manifests a propensity to the perceptions of the reasonable person adds an additional, complex, and socially volatile range of elasticity.

"Contact/conduct that manifests . . . a propensity . . . ." When Clinton first asked for conduct-based regulation, he seems to have had in mind only "prohibited conduct" — UCMJ sodomy. No serious proposal was that narrow, but White House apologetics — disingenuously or deviously — continued to pretend that all proposed policies reflected Clinton's conduct basis. Reno's Memo approving the New DOD Policy stated that it permitted conduct discharges only on the basis of "acts that *everyone* would regard as *explicitly sexual*,"even though it was attached to a New DOD Policy that spoke of conduct that a *reasonable person* would think *manifests a propensity!* [11] Meanwhile, Presi-

dent Clinton presented the freshly minted New DOD Policy to a military audience at Fort McNair as though "propensity" were no different from "intent" (WH4).

But, even the *Old* DOD Policy had foregone Clinton's purported narrow definition of homosexual conduct. The policy in place when Clinton took office had defined homosexual conduct more amply as same-sex bodily contacts intended to provide sexual gratification. The new language reaches still further, to encompass all bodily *contacts* that a reasonable person would suppose to *manifest a propensity.* According to the Training Manual issued by the DOD to explain the 1993 revisions, homosexual conduct thus defined includes the nonerotic but apparently excessively friendly contact of "two enlisted men holding hands in a secluded section of a public park" (DOD8). And military officials have interpreted this provision even more capaciously, to include any *conduct* that a reasonable person would think manifests a propensity.

The last move is truly startling. In testimony before the House Armed Services Committee, General Colin Powell indicated that military decision-makers would expand "*contacts*" to include "*conduct.*" When Representative Ike Shelton asked the Joint Chiefs how the New DOD Policy would apply to a servicemember who read gay magazines, frequented a gay bar, and marched in gay rights parades but engaged in no homosexual contacts, Powell answered: "What we are asking our commanders to do is not see any one of those items as a circuit breaker. [But] if all three [of those behaviors] occur, the commander has to start considering whether he is not dealing with someone who has a propensity. . . . What we would expect the commander to do is assemble all of the information" (Lancaster, "Joint Chiefs"). That is to say, an investigation can be initiated, and the burden to show no propensity can be shifted to the servicemember, if he or she never identifies as gay or engages in a same-sex bodily act or any other "acts" that the New DOD Policy regulates, but rather engages in conduct that a commander—applying his or her own cultural lexicon in sexual orientation matters—construes to indicate a deviant propensity.

It is hard to imagine *any* conduct that falls categorically outside the theoretical scope of this interpretation of the propensity clauses. Moreover, "assembl[ing] all of the information" and conducting a witchhunt are not really distinguishable in practice: Powell's answer states his view that, once a commander has detected any conduct that manifests a possible propensity, he or she can bypass "don't pursue" and launch an investigation. It was in response to Representative Jon L. Kyle's immediate objection that such inquiries were exactly what the text of the New DOD Policy prohibited that Aspin responded: "Under this policy, the commander is the arbiter of all gray area decisions. It's his judgment as to whether he's got credible information" justifying him in instituting separation proceedings (Lancaster, "Joint Chiefs").

Powell's construction of "contact" goes well beyond its conventional meaning, and should have been rejected by the White House. But instead it has permitted the DOD to promulgate regulations that reject Powell's specific claim but simultaneously authorize commanders to initiate investigations on similar information. Commanders are instructed that "associational activity such as going to a gay bar, possessing or reading homosexual publications, associating with known homosexuals, or marching in a gay rights rally in civilian clothes" does not "provide evidence of homosexual conduct." But discharge proceedings can commence when "a reliable person states that he or she observed behavior that amounts to a non-verbal statement by a member that he or she is a homosexual or bisexual—i.e., behavior that a reasonable person would believe intended to convey the statement that the member . . . has a propensity to engage in homosexual acts" (DODD2/a E.4, F.3; DODD3/a E.4, F.3). I'll defer for the moment the leaven added to this lump by the reliable, reasonable person; for now it is enough to note that same-sex contacts are rendered unnecessary when *any conduct* is construed as a statement that contacts might occur.

Doubtless some commanders adhere to the White House's narrow reading of conduct that manifests a propensity, but they are not constrained to do so. They are free to give the provision its broadest meaning, and to initiate investigations and separation proceedings on the basis of conduct that makes them think a servicemember is gay. Indeed, once a commander thinks a subordinate is gay, he or she can designate almost anything that person does as a signifier of a propensity and thus as "homosexual conduct": in the new tautology of anti-gay enforcement, *homosexual conduct has become the conduct of homosexuals.*

Powell acknowledged this tautology when he told the Senate Armed Forces Committee that marching in a gay rights parade would not constitute homosexual conduct because heterosexuals do it: "I don't know how we could say to a heterosexual servicemember that if they chose to go to a gay rights parade, either to observe it or to make a statement about their view of it, but they, themselves, are heterosexual, that we should tell them they can't do that, or that we should take some action against them for doing it" (Cong.2).

Aspin made the same definitional move:

> Sen. McCain: So — so what you're saying is that in — in — but yet, being in a homosexual parade, marching in a gay rights rally in civilian clothes is not homosexual conduct.
>
> Sec. Aspin: Because a person might be a heterosexual who's in favor of gay rights and attends the gay parade, yes. (Cong.2, see also Kavanagh)

Far from regulating homosexual conduct *and not* homosexual status, and even more than ascribing status on the basis of conduct, the conduct definition in the 1993 revisions invites commanders to ascribe *conduct* on the basis of *status.*

Less conceptually sophisticated are a number of interpretive devices that allow military decision-makers to discover evidence of bodily contacts notwithstanding "don't ask" and "don't pursue." The will to transform statements cases into contacts cases is apparent in two internal memoranda, neither of them intended to be circulated to the public, promulgated by Navy and Air Force lawyers. The Navy's appellate litigation section (dubbed "Code 34") advises officers involved in separation proceedings how to exploit its "experiences in 'statements' cases vice [i.e., versus] 'acts' cases" (Navy1). In a similar memorandum, the Air Force Judge Advocate General (JAG) exhorts commanders to bring cases under the protection of the Ninth Circuit's concession in *Meinhold v. Department of Defense* that separations for conduct are not unconstitutional: "To the extent possible, consistent with the facts, separations should be initiated based upon acts or marriages; even *Meinhold* supports discharges based upon acts" (AF1).

Both the Navy Code 34 Memo and the Air Force JAG Memo exploit a crucial delegation of discretionary authority to military enforcers. The Statute and the Implementing Regulations fail to provide servicemembers with enforceable protections against inquisitorial searches for conduct evidence. The DOD's only efforts to inform commanders in any detail about when they may or may not initiate investigations under the Statute appear in " 'Guidelines for Fact-Finding Inquiries into Homosexual Conduct," a document that repeatedly states that it creates no enforceable rights. The Guidelines specifically disable servicemembers from raising any procedural objections when commanders fail to follow them. That is to say, "don't ask" and "don't pursue" have been negotiated out of law and into the range of military discretion.

The Guidelines and other soft regulations stipulate that "*Commanders* . . . shall . . . decide whether an inquiry is warranted" (DODD2/a A.1; DODD3/a A.1; emphasis added); that "Investigations shall be limited to the factual circumstances directly relevant to the specific allegations" (DODI2/b; see also DODD2/a A.3; DODD3/a A.3) and that "At any given point of the inquiry, the commander or appointed inquiry official must be able clearly and specifically to explain which grounds for separation he or she is attempting to verify and how the information being collected relates to those specific separation grounds" (DODD2/a D.4; DODD3/a D.4).

But the Code 34 memorandum contradicts these constraints on investigators, instructing officers to *"Be creative.* Where the case is premised on a statement alone, the recorder should attempt to find evidence to corroborate the statement and to sustain the presumption flowing logically from the statement. In terms of hearing preparation, the goal of the recorder is to build the strongest case possible." Officers are instructed to leave no stone unturned in seeking a conduct basis: "Although a statement alone may constitute a prima facie case, a recorder should present the board with additional evidence demonstrating that a discharge is warranted by the unequivocal desire of the respondent to commit homosexual acts. For some specific ideas, call Code 34." If the Guidelines direct investigators to verify statements and stop there, the Code 34 Memo authorizes wide-ranging searches for conduct evidence on the merest supposition that it might or must exist.[12]

Similarly, the Air Force JAG Memo advises officers that "The purpose of the inquiry is not to discover evidence of homosexual acts or to ferret out other homosexuals in the military. If acts or other military members are discovered during the proper course of the investigation, however, appropriate action may be taken" (AF1).[13] The "proper course of the investigation" is quite ample: the attached Guidelines direct commanders to ask questions about *other statements* (e.g., "Whom has he told he is a homosexual?"; "Has the member told any of his family members?"); questions that might produce evidence of conduct ("If the member used certain terms, such as 'homosexual orientation' or 'propensity,' ask the following question: 'What did the member mean by 'homosexual orientation' or 'propensity?'' "; "Can [the member] explain what he means [by a 'propensity to engage in homosexual acts']?"; "How does he know he has a 'homosexual orientation' and/or 'propensity'?"; "Has the member been dating anybody (opposite or same sex)? How frequently has the member dated? How recently? How can these people be contacted?"). The inquiry probes the servicemember's political associations: "Did the member belong to any homosexual student organizations at school? If so, which? How can other members of the organization, who knew of his membership, be contacted?" And officers are encouraged to seek to ascertain whether servicemembers are really gay by interviewing "parents and siblings" (AF3).

The Marine Corps pursues with equally unbridled investigative discretion. In the late summer of 1993, when the Statute was in the planning stages, the Officer in Charge of the Marine Corps Legal Service Support Section issued a memorandum that created vast "pursuit" powers for Defense Criminal Investigative Organizations (DCIOs)—powers that have since been used in at least one systematic conduct witch-hunt. The Marine Memo, addressed to the section that provides assigned counsel to servicemembers being investigated for criminal sexual conduct, requires officers to delay assigning counsel until servicemembers have been detained for ten days or formally charged, and orders Marine lawyers to do nothing that could create an attorney/client privilege until they have been officially authorized to do so (MC1). This memorandum supported a recent witch-hunt at the Marine installation on Okinawa, in which servicemembers suspected of being gay, deprived of their *Miranda* right to counsel, confessed to violations of the UCMJ sodomy statute (CP14). During this ten-day window, DCIOs can ask virtually any questions they wish, and, according to the Servicemembers Legal Defense Network's 1996 report on enforcement of the Statute, that is exactly what they have done.

Military discretion to construe conduct grounds broadly and to engage in wide-ranging investigations once such grounds are established is so broad that it can eliminate any "progress" imputed to the 1993 revisions. A commander who notes with suspicious displeasure that a male subordinate has marched in a gay rights parade in civilian clothes, made a memorial gift for a male friend who died of AIDS, and spoken in support of Clinton's reforms can deem these acts to be conduct that manifests a propensity. Even though no *contacts* are involved, the servicemember will find nothing in the regulations that allows him to challenge the commander's decision to open an investigation. The investigator can then contact college roommates, parents, and siblings seeking evidence of homosexual contacts, coming-out statements, or any other evidence that would manifest a propensity. Even if the investigation turns up no new evidence, it is nevertheless the servicemember's burden to show that he has *no* propensity; and, where the Navy Code 34 Memo is being followed, any evidence of pro-gay sentiment can come in to impeach his proof.

The Servicemembers Legal Defense Network, the premier gay-rights advocacy organization representing servicemembers harmed by military anti-gay policy, has argued to the White House that the exercise of discretion I have just detailed lawlessly violates rights that servicemembers acquired in the 1993 revisions. To do so they not only promoted the Guidelines from their apparent provisional status as *advice* to *law,* but also sought to drive a semiotic wedge between *status* and *conduct.* Legal advocates are under rhetorical constraints that make such an assertion of a right to status protection almost *de rigueur,* but a critical understanding of the 1993 revisions must acknowledge that both the status/conduct distinction and the claim to institutionally acknowledged rights are more problematic than that.

A semiotic imbrication of status with conduct and conduct with status occurs at every relevant procedural moment, from the legislative debates to the daily business of enforcement. Because line officers have the discretion to manipulate that semiosis, the new policy's center of gravity is not servicemembers' procedural "rights" but the substantive generation of military anti-gay culture. On that score, the "reasonable person" feature is even more invidious than the conduct grounds.

". . . to a reasonable person . . . ." Joint Chiefs Chair Colin Powell was right to worry that the new policy might work harm to a straight servicemember who marched in a gay-pride parade. The unpredictability produced by the volatility of the new policy's "conduct" terms produces an anxiety that is ultimately less concerned with homosexual than with heterosexual status. The new dynamics of heterosexual immunity and heterosexual vulnerability are neatly packed into the crucial novelty unveiled by the New DOD Policy and retained by the Statute: the definition of "homosexual acts" to include "bodily contacts which *a reasonable person* would understand to demon-

strate a propensity or intent to engage in" an erotic, same-sex bodily contact.

It appears that the "reasonable person" provision was inserted into the New DOD Policy just before Aspin announced it. The only textual precedent I have been able to find for this innovation is Nunn's third principle, which provided for discharge of a servicemember whose acts *demonstrate* a propensity to engage in homosexual conduct. Here was a rudimentary recognition that sexual-orientation identity requires not only a human object but also an observer, a subject with the power and authority to ascribe homosexual identity. Someone—I don't profess to know who—significantly upgraded this insight at some moment between Nunn's speech on July 15, 1993, and Aspin's announcement on July 19, by indexing Nunn's "demonstrat[ion]" to the hermeneutic practices of a "reasonable person." The authorship of this revision is a dog that didn't bark in the night: the lack of any trace in the textual record of a dispute over it suggests that the players remaining at the table when it was drafted shared, or maintained their own, reasons for liking it.

The "reasonable person" feature makes the interpretive standpoint of heterosexual personhood an indispensable reference point for enforcement. But heterosexuals gain this authority and immunity at the price of considerable status instability. No one can be sure that he or she is identical to the "reasonable person." Though self-identified heterosexuals can hope that their own behavioral hermeneutics will be inscribed into the lexicon of the reasonable person, no self-identified heterosexual can be sure of conforming consistently to the heterosexual protocols stipulated by the "reasonable person." Indeed, no self-identified heterosexual can ever be sure he or she even knows what those protocols *are*. To the extent that even the most firmly heterosexual servicemember apprehends a possible gap between his or her own social understandings and those attributed by others to the "reasonable person," heterosexual reason will be anxious reason.

Indeed, given the amplification of conduct by propensity, given the rich homosocial practices of comradeship in the military, and given the armed services' history of attributing lesbianism to women servicemembers on grounds of their supposed gender nonconformity (see Benecke and Dodge; Britton and Williams; and Karst), few servicemembers can possibly be so unambiguously straight that they will never wonder whether a reasonable person might construe their actions as homosexual conduct. All servicemembers living under the Statute must ask themselves what the "reasonable person" would think of their actions. They must learn to read their social world from the perspective of that observer. They will never be sure that their readings are right, because the reasonable person's reasonable constructions will be persistently in flux as the culture of a homo/hetero distinction is worked out in each branch of service, indeed in each unit, each year, each month, each day.

This introjection of the reasonable person is a particularly vivid example of what Michael Warner has called *heteronormativity*. The reasonable person merges the Aristotelian conception of the "golden mean," the norm as the normatively *good*, with the actuarial conception of the "average," the "statistical mean," the "norm" as an ever-moving, socially invisible midpoint of a population's variability (Hacking, *Taming* 160–69). François Ewald reminds us that "The norm is the group's observation of itself. . . . A norm is a self-referential standard of measurement for a given group. . . . [Norms are] inconstant, almost by definition" (155–56). He indicates that where norms provide social order "there is no need to impose a law on the living in order to ensure regularity in their behavior" (158).

Ewald predicts that, when norms supplant rigid, formal, inflexible rules, the product is a social order that is persistently regular and that yet nevertheless holds out permanent promises to no one: "Abnormality is defined as a handicap or inability. It no longer refers to a natural quality or property of being; instead, it signals some aspect of the group's relation to itself. The relationship between the normal and the abnormal thus becomes an unstable threshold" (158). The reasonable person in the 1993 revisions to military anti-gay policy operates as just such a norm: to the extent that individual heterosexual persons approximate it, they accumulate its value, and yet, because it is always on the move, they can never capture it. Heteronormativity under the 1993 revisions holds out the lure of tremendous conceptual and hermeneutic authority at the price of persistent personal anxiety.

How will the reasonable person read the world? Guidelines issued to help commanders enforce the 1993 revisions resolutely refuse to answer that question (of course). But their various refusals insist that, whatever turns out to be the right answer, the reasonable person will reach it not only by observing acts of same-sex sex, but also by consulting immense reserves of cultural detail about the sexual orientation "statuses." Consider one example. When Aspin presented the New DOD Policy to Congress, he supplied Guidelines that provided an example of conduct that manifests a propensity: "handholding or kissing in most circumstances." "Most" sets up a presumption that same-sex handholding or kissing does indeed demonstrate a propensity; "circumstances" delegates the decision whether the presumption is defeated to the reasonable person.

This all seems to be quite mollifying common sense, but even Aspin's innocuous example indicated that the "reasonable person" is a specular location from which conduct that does and that does not manifest a propensity varies depending on "circumstances" that can only be called the semiotics of status. What are the "circumstances" of bodily acts? Which circumstances support the presumption and which defeat it? To answer these questions the reasonable person must draw on deep reservoirs of cultural information about homosexual and heterosexual persons: the expectation that same-sex handholding is aberrant, except in the rare circumstances where it is perfectly normal; the different norms that might allow sexual orientation to be deduced from two *women* holding hands as opposed to two *men* doing the same thing; and so on. Answering these questions requires reference to ideas about who homosexuals are and how their repertoires of social behavior differ from those available to and used by heterosexuals. It requires reference to what the 1993 debates designate as status, and well beyond that to the culture of homo/hetero differentiation.

To the extent that the reasonable person operates as a law-like norm, each servicemember must anticipate and heed these capacious, open-ended cultural discernments.

That's bad enough, but in the regime of the reasonable person things can be even worse.

Attempting to clean up Aspin's example, the DOD issued a training manual, spelling out some "circumstances" in which the reasonable person could say that handholding manifests a propensity: imagine (1) two (2) enlisted (3) men, (4) both (5) off duty and (6) wearing civilian clothes, (7) detected by (8) an officer (9) holding hands while (10) walking (11) alone in an (12) isolated (13) wooded (14) public (15) park (DOD8). Virtually every numbered detail asks the reasonable person to draw on his (or her?) own database of personhood norms. For instance, some but not all people assume that (5) most single men limited to scarce leisure time spend it on erotic adventures; that (9) most men don't hold hands with other men; and that (12–15) most men who touch each other in the half-privacy of public parks are there to have sex. Even the detail that the two men are enlisted draws on cultural information: the manual's typological *mise-en-scène* is, we are asked to understand, an affectionate or at least entirely consensual relationship; if the hands being held belonged to an enlisted man and an officer, military anti-gay ideology would have silently stipulated that the relationship was unavoidably coercive. Everything about the construction and interpretation of this scene depends upon information not about conduct alone, but about the attribution of status.

Lest commanders think that this wealth of circumstantial detail and concatenated inference will be needed to support the reasonable person's conclusion that these enlisted men have a propensity to homosexual conduct, the training manual instructs them that its sylvan scene "indicates" not merely a propensity but "*a homosexual act*" —the deed itself. Far thinner circumstances, supported by far fewer cultural suppositions about homosexual and heterosexual persons, would make it reasonable to detect a propensity.

To measure the extent to which the reasonable person's detection of a propensity vaporizes conduct and substitutes for it not even the solidities of status but the anxious mutabilities of ascriptive identification, it might help to apply the new DOD regulations to an instance of conduct alleged in 1981. In proceedings under the then-brand-new

Old DOD Policy, the Army sought to prove that Perry Watkins had engaged in homosexual conduct. Its proof was the testimony of PFC David P. Valley, who "testified that [Watkins] asked him if he'd like to move into [Watkins's] apartment with him and that [Watkins] used to come by the mailroom and stare at Valley" (*Watkins A* 257). Valley also testified "that he was not sure [Watkins] had been making an advance toward him." "In addition, Valley admitted to being prejudiced against black people"—Watkins was African American—"and against homosexuals, having once had a bad experience with a homosexual, and related that he had been disciplined once by a board of which [Watkins] was a member." Watkins's hearing board and the Navy's Legal Advisor concluded that these assertions provided sufficient evidence to support a conduct-based discharge. The District Court disagreed with them (*Watkins A* 257).

What would the outcome be if the same allegations were made today, under the Statute? The DOD's amended "Guidelines for Fact-Finding Inquiries into Homosexual Conduct" would instruct a commander to ask not whether

Watkins has engaged in same-sex bodily contacts but whether he can be charged with "(1) language or behavior that (2) a reasonable person would believe (3) was intended to convey the statement (4) that [Watkins] engages in, attempts to engage in, or has a propensity to engage in homosexual acts." In 1981 the District Court thought that Valley's prejudice against homosexuals and his bitter memory of a "bad experience with a homosexual" impeached his credibility. Today, after Congress and the Department of Justice have described precisely this homophobic anxiety as an aversion not to persons but to homosexual acts, Valley's anti-gay animus and his anxiety about his own sexual orientation are quite plausibly the constitutive features of the reasonable person.

A commander seeking to enforce the 1993 revisions to the max could commit Watkins to separation proceedings on the basis of Valley's evidence; because "the commander is the arbiter of all gray area decisions," including decisions about what a reasonable person might think, his decision would be unreviewable. It would shift the burden of persuasion to Watkins, whose discharge would be mandatory if he could not prove to his hearing board that he lacked a propensity.

How does one prevent people like Valley from construing friendly gestures as homosexual recruitment? *Very carefully*. The reasonable person's detection of a propensity to commit homosexual acts, when it operates as the hetero-norm I have described here, defeats Janet Reno's and DOJ lawyers' most vaulting claims for the New DOD Policy. Far from regulating conduct *and not* status, the "reasonable person" device depends on both to make the anti-gay policy a social mechanism for identity production and ascription. Far from introducing a cool actuarial model of behavioral propensity that adventitiously disadvantages a status-based social group, it generates the very pressures that make the group — and indeed, the very idea of sexual-orientation identity — a social and psychological necessity. Far from replacing value judgments with statistical observation, it requires servicemembers to incorporate, as their own lexicon of social interpretation, the hermeneutic practices of the homophobe: it goes well beyond reflecting popular prejudices, to produce and require them.

Conclusion

Attacking the new military policy on constitutional grounds, several servicemembers' lawyers have insisted that their clients suffered discrimination based on their status, not their conduct. They have represented their clients not as people against whom no sexual crimes have been proven, but as people who do not and would not engage in "homosexual conduct." Where a servicemember client is truly and contentedly celibate, this is fine. But (as Diane Mazur insists) the argument is an insult to the personal sexual dignity of most servicemember clients, and (as Michael Bronski insists) it abandons a normatively crucial project of any pro-gay movement: building a social consensus that homosexual erotic acts are good.

Telling truth to power requires that gay advocates deal forthrightly with the empirical and normative validity of the propensity clauses' actuarial premise: that self-identified homosexuals *do* engage in more same-sex erotic conduct than those who identify otherwise. (It's a tough job, but *someone* has to do it.) Accepting — indeed, revelling in—this premise, however, doesn't weaken any fully accurate attack on the new military anti-gay policy.

The actuarial model of a propensity is only one of the two crucial premises of the propensity clauses: the other is the psychometric model of a propensity. To be sure, these premises are contradictory: ascribing a propensity on the basis of a statistical, impersonal, nominal metaphysics is quite a different matter from doing the same thing on the basis of a personality-based, individualizing, and realist metaphysics. But as we have seen, the two premises go hand in hand throughout the development, enforcement, and justification of the propensity presumption and the accompanying rebuttal burden. The two premises (one corresponding with conduct, the other with status) are contradictory yet mutually requisite to make the whole apparatus work.

To put the same point in the more general terms of status and conduct, the ominous legal artistry of the new military anti-gay policy elaborated *Hardwick*'s permission to criminalize "homosexual sodomy" into a capacious and flexible semiotic and procedural system for ascribing status on the basis of conduct and conduct on the basis of status. Anti-gay practices developed under the 1993 revisions do not target status or conduct: rather, they persistently render status a sign of conduct and vice versa. The overarching mechanism of the new military anti-gay policy is not status *or* conduct, but a newly volatile, artifactual relationship between them.

To describe the policy, then, as a regulation of conduct-not-status, or of status-not-conduct, is to distort it. The Department of Justice and the many courts that have defended the policy on grounds that it targets homosexual conduct and not homosexual status (e.g., *Able D* 1296–99; *Thomasson B* 927–34, *Watson* 1407, *Richenberg A* 1312–13, *Selland II* 265–66) describe it so inaccurately that it is hard to credit their good faith. At the same time, pro-gay arguments insisting that the new policy is status–*and not conduct*–based are equally off the mark. Even though they have been able to persuade some judges to adopt their view (e.g., *Able C* 974; *Able A* 1043; *Holmes A* 1527–28, 1535, *Richenberg B* 173–74 [Arnold, J., dissenting] — note that these are all reversed or dissenting opinions), the sheer facts of the policy's dynamics are against them. It is the new military policy's systematic structure, not any one of its elements, that makes it what it is. If it is to be justified, it needs justification *as a system.* If it is to be attacked, it should be attacked *as a system.*

Let's assume that judges confront rather than avoid the status/conduct complexity of the policy. The constitutional terminology under which they would adjudicate this conflict would permit them to come out either way. But the glib adoption of the conduct-not-status description of the policy and the equally glib invocation of *Hardwick* would be unavailable; and so attacks on the policy would be correspondingly more weighty. Courts would have to confront the proliferation of status-based discriminations in the Statute; particularly since Congress introduced several of them in order to eliminate conduct-only improvements proposed by the Clinton administration, courts would have to understand these discriminations to be *intentional.* The actuarial model of a propensity does not magically transform all of these status-inflecting provisions into conduct regulation. Courts could say that the "don't tell" rules regulate speech according to its content, without excuse when the content itself—homosexual status—is expressly permitted. (Two judges have done so: see *Able E* 965; *Holmes B* 1138–40 [Reinhardt J., dissenting].) Courts could hold that the military regulations discriminate when they impute a propensity on the basis of some speech acts but not others that are indistinguishable from them absent that imputation; and that they discriminate when they allow heterosexual identification but not homosexual identification to rebut presumptions arising from the same conduct. (Several judges have done so: see *Holmes* 1528–31; *Meinhold C* 1478 n. 11; see also cp5; cp6.)

Courts could then say that these discriminations are so irrational that they fail even minimal constitutional review. They could say that it is irrational to protect against conduct-based harm to military effectiveness when homosexuals engage in the conduct but not when heterosexuals do, or when open homosexuals rather than closeted ones commit it. (Two appellate judges have adopted this view: see *Holmes B* 1139 [Reinhardt, J., dissenting]; *Philips B* 1435 [Fletcher, J., dissenting].) Since this conduct goal of the policy is fundamental to its entire structure, a court that holds it irrational eliminates all justification for the entire discriminatory apparatus.

Courts could also reject all the rationales offered to support military anti-gay policy as themselves irrational. First, they could observe that unit cohesion, privacy in the barracks and the showers, and sexual tranquility are eroded, not promoted, by the policy's joint legitimation of servicemembers' homophobic sensibilities and of secretive homosexual presence in the military. (Several trial judges have adopted this point: see *Holmes A* 1531–32; *Thorne A* 1371–72; *Able C* 978.) Then they could say that, stripped of their contradictory content, these justifications are nothing but accommodations to existing anti-gay animus among servicemembers. Courts could even reject these rationales as pretextual: they could see anti-gay animus in *Congress*.[1] Wherever the animus lies, it is not a constitutionally legitimate ground for state action. The Supreme Court has held that "[p]rivate biases may be outside the reach of the law, but the law cannot, directly or indirectly, give them effect" (*Palmore* 433); "mere negative attitudes . . . are not permissible bases" for state-sponsored discrimination (*Cleburne* 448). And citing these principles, the Supreme Court has recently held, in a crucial decision invalidating Colorado's anti-gay Amendment 2, that "if the constititutional conception of 'equal protection of the laws' means anything it must at the very least mean that a bare . . . desire to harm a politically unpopular group cannot constitute a legitimate governmental interest" (*Romer* 634, quoting *United States Department of Agriculture v. Moreno* 534; for decisions pursuing this critique, see *Holmes A* 19–21; *Able C* 980; *Able E* 858–61; see also *Philips B* 1434–38 [Fletcher, J., dissenting]).

But there is a deeper irrationality underlying the new military anti-gay policy that constitutional analysis lacks the tools to notice. Having created the propensity apparatus in order to justify discharge based on coming-out statements, the policy vastly expanded the conduct grounds for discharge. Commanders have unreviewable discretion to initiate proceedings against servicemembers who have engaged in any acts that a "reasonable person" would think manifests a propensity to engage in same-sex sexual conduct. Because this decision cannot be reviewed, the commander has the ultimate call on what a "reasonable person" would think. And because it is tied to the norms of sexual performativity in the commander's unit, there can be no law on this subject: *anything* could be conduct that manifests a propensity. Self-identified homosexuals are in danger under this kind of regime, certainly; but so are people who think of themselves as thoroughly heterosexual. Not only that, but the more vigorously the policy is enforced, the more dangerously volatile becomes the ascriptive culture it promotes. That is, if the policy actually works well to promote the expressed interests of the homophobic servicemembers whom Congress heeded with such sycophantic eagerness in its 1993 hearings, it will endanger them. Their anxiety will sharpen their need for aggressive and voracious anti-gay enforcement, which will increase their anxiety, which will increase their need for anti-gay enforcement, and so on.

Kendall Thomas ("Shower/Closet") and Judith Butler have described the new military anti-gay policy as a massive inscription into law of the paranoid psychic and scopic structure of hetereosexuality. Seen as *discrimination,* this structure is difficult to describe: *no one benefits* because *no one belongs* in any extrinsic way to an advantaged or disadvantaged group; heterosexuality, not the group "heterosexuals," is the chief beneficiary. If courts see this structure at all, they are likely to see it as a policy choice, either a deep, self-policing value-based decision of a majority to constrain itself to a sexuality it deems socially, but not erotically, desirable or a mistake that the powerful majority that made it can unmake at will. Under either view, courts are likely to see themselves as institutionally incompetent to address this deep, deeply characteristic, and alarming feature of the new policy: the problem will have to be addressed through political, not judicial, action.

The military policy revisions of 1993 thus present the potential for generating a crisis. If their most central and characteristic evils can be addressed only in the political sphere, that sphere may well be disabled to address it by the policy itself. If courts *do* say that the policy is constitutionally sound, and if they say so without any proviso that judicial deference to military policy motivates them, then they will have approved the policy as a model for official anti-gay discrimination elsewhere. A formalization of private discrimination could follow. If government and private discrimination modeled on the military policy become widespread, they will generate rather than allay homophobia, and produce their own unrepealability. We are, happily, many contingencies away from this frightening world. It seems, then, to be a good moment for people identified as heterosexual who support or accept the policy to think about what they are doing. If they adopted the 1993 revisions to military anti-gay policy out of self-interest, they have simply made a mistake, and they should unmake it. If they adopted the new policy out of a self-constraining value choice, as a way of imposing heterosexuality by law on themselves, then they have engaged in conduct that manifests a propensity. Failure to repeal the policy, in either case, is an ongoing act of bad faith.

Notes

Introduction

1   I will refer to *Bowers v. Hardwick* as *Hardwick* in order to avoid
    confusion with *Shahar v. Bowers,* in which Robin Joy Shahar un-
    successfully sued Georgia Attorney General Michael Bowers (yes,
    the same Bowers) for dismissing her on the ground of her partici-
    pation in a same-sex marriage ceremony.

2   For examples of the former in which there was evidence of actual
    conduct, see *Matthews; Dronenberg;* and, under the new policy,
    Philips. These are vastly outnumbered by cases rejecting equal-
    protection claims by inferring conduct from status: for nonmili-
    tary cases see *Equality Foundation B* 267 and *High Tech Gays B*
    571–74; for cases challenging pre-1993 military policy see *Steffan A*
    123; *Steffan E* 684; *Ben-Shalom II B* 464–65; and *Woodward* 1076.

    For cases holding that anti-gay discrimination was based on
    status, not conduct, and thus could gain special scrutiny under
    the equal-protection clause, see *Jantz* 1546–47; *High Tech Gays A*
    1371–72; *High Tech Gays C* 379–80 (Canby and Norris, J., dissent-
    ing from denial of rehearing *en banc);* and *Equality Foundation A*
    440. Former military policy was sometimes deemed unconstitu-
    tional under this rationale: *Watkins C* 714, 716–20 (Norris, J., con-
    curring); *Steffan B* 76; *Steffan D* 70; *Meinhold C* 1479, 1478; *Pruitt*
    1164; *Cammermeyer* 920; *Elzie* 442; *Selland I* 17; *Dahl.* Valdes
    added academic support to this line of cases, which can probably

be traced to Justice Blackmun's dissent in *Hardwick*, with its eloquent invocation of homosexual "personhood" (205–6).

3   I anticipated that people would hesitate to take the blame for a policy so evidently coauthored at many stages of sometimes brutal negotiation, and so evidently rife with incoherences, contradictions, and openings to unfair application. I was surprised when sociologist Charles Moscos stepped forward to take credit for it. His claim to be "the" architect of "the" policy (Talk of the Nation 35) is called into question by the heterogeneous textual history of the 1993 revisions as it appears in detail below.

1   *The Negotiations and the Players*

1   The bibliography provides citations to these documents as follows: (1) for the Old DOD Policy, see section I.A.2; (2) for the Interim Policy, see section I.B.1; (3) for the New DOD Policy, see section I.B.3; (4) for the Statute, see section I.A.1; and (5) for the Implementing Regulations, see I.A.3. See the headnote to the bibliography for help in finding other documents.

2   At one point the *New York Times* could report on the Joint Chiefs' involvement only by relying on triple hearsay: see Friedman, "Legal Concerns." For other scanty reports of the Joint Chiefs' role in the negotiations, see Schmitt, "White House"; Schmitt, n.t.; Friedman, "Clinton Is Said"; Friedman, "Accord," and Carlson.

2   *Clinton is to Conduct as Congress is to Status*

1   See DODI1; see also Byrne 56. According to Byrne's summary of military rules before 1993, commanders who had evidence of most UCMJ violations had a broad range of options: they could dismiss the matter entirely, impose administrative sanctions short of separation or criminal punishment, impose nonjudicial punishment, or continue the action by conducting further investigation themselves or referring the charge to an independent investigative service. They were required, however, to refer all really serious matters, specifically including "perverted sexual activity such as

homosexuality," for criminal investigation by the Defense Criminal Investigative Organization of their own service. Consensual same-sex sodomy, a felony under the UCMJ, was thus taken out of commanders' hands and committed to authorities with power to institute criminal charges (Byrne 55–56).

2   Separation Regulations Part 1, K.l.a.3 provide that "[a] member may be separated" for "commission of a serious offense": male-female fellatio would be covered by this section, which makes separation discretionary. Separation Regulations Part 1, K.1.c provide that "misconduct involving homosexuality shall be processed under Section H"—that is, the regulations directly addressed to homosexuality. Section H under the Old DOD Policy provided that a servicemember found to have engaged in homosexual acts, to have stated that he or she was homosexual, or to have married **135** a person of the same sex "*shall* be separated." The new Implementing Regulations retain the mandatory rather than discretionary nature of commanders' power in cases involving homosexual misconduct: commanders are required to initiate discharge when they receive "credible information" of homosexual conduct and can avoid a sanction of separation only in stated exceptional circumstances (DODD2 H.1.b, 4.a, 4.b(l), 4.d, 4.g).

3   The answer was: "Yes, sir. Sir, you're not supposed to ask, but since you did, yes, sir, I am" (Miles 65).

4   If "coming out" is a political act, it should be understood as political speech; and prohibiting it to gay men, lesbians, and bisexuals while permitting others to profess heterosexual identity *ad libitum* is a matter of First Amendment *and* equal protection concern. For discussions of these points—which somehow have escaped most federal judges—see *Able E* 965; *Holmes B*, 1138–40 (Reinhardt, J., dissenting); *Gay Law Students* 488; Cole and Eskridge; Hunter; Halley, "The Politics of the Closet."

3   *But Everyone Agrees on the Propensity Clauses*

1   The following analysis of the social function of actuarial concepts has been informed by Simon 790–91; Feeley and Simon, "Actuarial Justice" and "The New Penology"; Hacking, *Taming*

of Chance, "How Should We Do," and "Making Up People"; Danziger, "Statistical Method" and "The Methodological Imperative in Psychology"; Bulmer, Bales, and Sklar; Asad; and Ewald.

2   The Reno Memo is hard to obtain. Just for the record, here is the entire passage: "[T]he policy implements the distinction between 'status' and 'conduct' that you drew in your January 29 directive. Most important in this regard is the treatment of statements of homosexuality or bisexuality as creating 'a rebuttable presumption that the service member is engaging in homosexual acts or has a propensity or intent to do so.' First Amendment problems would arise if the policy proscribed certain speech, in and of itself, because of disapproval of the content or the viewpoint expressed. This approach provides much clearer authority than did the pre-January policy for the argument that the Department of Justice has been making persuasively to the courts up to this point that a member who credibly disproved any intent or propensity to commit physical acts would not be subject to separation. The new policy suggests a meaningful opportunity to rebut the presumption flowing from statements of homosexuality. As a result, the Department of Justice will be better able to argue that the policy is not directed at speech or expression itself, and that any burdens in those respects are incidental to the achievement of an important government interest."

3   A propensity is "An innate inclination; a tendency" (*American Heritage Dictionary of the English Language*); "an often intense natural inclination or preference" (*Webster's Ninth New Collegiate Dictionary*); "an inclination or tendency" (*Concise Oxford Dictionary of Current English*); "a natural inclination or bent" (*Barnhart Dictionary of Etymology*). The *Oxford English Dictionary* indicates that interiority and naturalness have been defining features of "propensity" from the earliest uses of the word in English: "1. The quality or character of being 'propense' or inclined to something; inclination, disposition, tendency, bent. . . . a. Disposition or inclination to some action, course of action, habit, etc.; bent of mind or nature. . . . b. Disposition to favour, benefit or associate oneself with some person, party, etc.; favourable inclination, good will. . . . c. Tendency or liability to some physical condition or

action (1660 SHARROCK *Vegetables* 141 Why have those plants . . . a propensity of sending forth roots?)."

4   The pervasive adoption of language from the MWG Report is all the more striking because of the complete failure of the RAND Report, also commissioned by Aspin, to have any noticeable impact. The RAND Report concluded that lesbians and gay men could serve openly in the military without reducing combat effectiveness or unit cohesion, provided there was strong leadership at the top supporting the new policy. It concluded that "the presence of a known homosexual is unlikely to undermine task cohesion," which is, in turn, "what drives successful performance" (30). It also concluded that a policy ending discrimination on the basis of sexual orientation in the military would work if "[t]he message of policy change [is] clear and . . . consistently communicated from the top" (39). The RAND Report contributes no language to any publicly proposed policy. Press reports confirm that the MWG Report was pivotal, and the RAND report entirely marginal, throughout the process. See Schmitt, "A Compromise," "Pentagon Keeps Silent," and "Pentagon Speeds Plan"; "A Retreat on Gay Soldiers"; and Lippman, "Pentagon Studies Conflict."

Neither report was made available to the public until late in August 1993, more than a month after Clinton and Aspin had issued their proposal. Inasmuch as the RAND Report critiques rather than supports Aspin's policy, and inasmuch as the MWG Report manifests the will of military leaders to obtain an absolute ban on all "homosexuality" in uniform, withholding these reports until they had lost anything but archival value kept the public in the dark not only about the full range of options on the table, but about the stakes of the inside players.

5   Watkins's case was litigated as a statement case, despite a 1968 affidavit in which he admitted having engaged in homosexual acts with two other servicemen. The Ninth Circuit panel concluded that the Army denied Watkins reenlistment on the grounds of his statements because a heterosexual soldier involved in the same acts would not be excludable (*Watkins B* 1436–37), and subsequent proceedings did not disturb this decision to ignore the evidence of Watkins's acts.

6   Technically, inasmuch as the underlying "fact" and the "presumption" it supports focus entirely on whether Ben-Shalom was "a homosexual," she was offered the opportunity not to rebut a presumption but to deny an allegation.

7   The district court had held that "the presumption must be, and it is rational for the Navy to believe, that plaintiff could one day have acted on his *preferences* in violation of regulations prohibiting such conduct" (*Steffan C* 13; emphasis added). Quoting this passage, the DOJ argued that it was rational to believe that Steffan " 'could one day have acted on his [*homosexual propensity*] in violation of regulations prohibiting such conduct" (CP11 15; emphasis added; bracketed insertion in original!).

8   DOJ attorneys and other drafters of the New DOD Policy took advantage of this opportunity. In an innovation, the New DOD Policy replaced "desires," the term that was causing the DOJ so much difficulty in the *Steffan* litigation, with "propensity." Whereas the Old DOD Policy defined "a homosexual" as a person who "engages in, desires to engage in, or intends to engage in homosexual acts," the New DOD Policy (which also refrained from defining homosexuals as persons) defined homosexual conduct to include a "statement by the servicemember that demonstrates a propensity or intent to engage in homosexual acts." The Statute, once again merging status with conduct, returned to persons but retained propensity: it defined a "homosexual" as "a person . . . who engages in, attempts to engage in, has a propensity to engage in, or intends to engage in homosexual acts" ((f)(1)).

9   See *Able D* 1296–99; *Watson* 1407; *Richenberg A* 1312–13; *Selland II* 265–66; *Thomasson B* 929, 932.

10 The "Seven Exhibits" are described in section I.D.3.e of the bibliography.

11 The complete passage can be read as a veiled threat to refuse to defend the policy should the military enforce it beyond these terms: "We can be confident that the prohibition on acts that everyone would regard as explicitly sexual would be sustained under existing case law" (Reno Memo). No one in the Clinton administration has delivered upon that threat, however.

12 The Code 34 Memo stipulates for similarly freewheeling lawyer-

ing in discharge hearings. Unenforceable directions in the DOD Guidelines state that "CREDIBLE INFORMATION [justifying a commander in opening an investigation] DOES NOT EXIST FOR EXAMPLE WHEN . . . the only information known concerns an associational activity such as going to a gay bar, possessing or reading homosexual publications, associating with known homosexuals, or marching in a gay rights rally in civilian clothes" (DODD2/a E.4; DODD3/a E.4). Nevertheless the Code 34 Memo instructs officers to "Point out on cross[-examination] that public denunciation of homosexual policies may be inconsistent with good military character. The wearing of one's uniform, or identifying oneself as a member of USN while visibly supporting homosexual interests may violate Uniform Regulations and the Standards of Conduct."

13   The supposed basis for asking questions about the servicemem-   **139**
ber's associations and conduct is the need to investigate the possibility that he or she must repay educational benefits under 10 U.S.C. § 2005, or has fraudulently stated that he or she is gay to evade service. The memorandum's precisionist suggestion that it seeks to avoid "don't ask" only in these special cases is specious: recoupment would be due from most officers, and any servicemember who has come out or engaged in "homosexual conduct" could be suspected of fraudulently seeking discharge.

Conclusion

1   This is a big step for a judge to take, and of all the ones outlined here it the least likely ever to be taken. Several judges, however, have come close. The status/conduct distinction supposedly drawn by the Statute has been called a mere "transmogrifi[cation]" and "nothing less than Orwellian" (*Able C* 975). The "professed focus on proscribed conduct" has been decried as a "camouflage," a "veneer," and "purely illusory" (*Holmes A* 1528). The resulting policy is "schizoid," "irrational and without substance," "fallacious," "arbitrary and unrealistic," the product of "dissembling," "patent disingenuousness," "[h]ypocrisy and deception" (*Holmes B*, 1137–39 [Reinhardt, J., dissenting]).

Bibliography

This bibliography was difficult to arrange for two reasons. First, I have depended on an unusually wide range of genres—from internal Navy memoranda to dictionaries, from law review articles to unpublished papers filed in litigation. Second, no one citation system adequately accommodates the details necessary to identify all these documents to the wide range of readers interested in this topic.

To make it easier to find particular documents, I've segmented the bibliography according to documents' institutional origins. To make citations in the text snappy, I've given documents shorthand titles. Some of these shorthand titles are acronymic; others are descriptive. Here is a list of the headings I've used, along with any acronymic titles that go with them. Where a document has a shorthand descriptive title, like "Reno Memo," the only way to find it is to look for its institutional author, in this case the Department of Justice (thus in I.B.2). When a shorthand title appears to designate a person, book, or media outlet, look for it in the section dedicated to Books, Articles, and Media (II).

I. Government Documents
    A. Statutes and Regulations
        1. Statutes
        2. Federal Regulations
        3. DOD (Department of Defense) Directives and Instructions (DODD and DODI)
        4. Army Regulations (Army Reg.)

B. Executive and Legislative Branches
   1. White House (WH1 through WH4)
   2. Department of Justice
   3. Department of Defense (DOD1 through DOD9)
   4. Congress (Cong.1 through Cong.7)
C. Military Branches
   1. Air Force (AF1 through AF3)
   2. Army (Army1)
   3. Marine Corps (MC1)
   4. Navy (Navy1)
D. Litigation and Other Advocacy
   1. Decisional Law
   2. Hearing Transcripts

   3. Court Papers and Other Advocacy Documents (CP1 through CP14)
      a. Able
      b. Hardwick
      c. Philips
      d. Steffan
      e. Watson (Chapman Declaration and Seven Exhibits)
      f. Advocacy to the Executive Branch
II. Books, Articles, and Media

Legal citations present a distinct challenge. Citations follow the *MLA Style Manual* to the extent that it can be adapted to legal citations. Where we have more than one court decision in a particular case, I've tagged them chronologically and alphabetically: *Able A, Able B,* and so on. In case citations, "U.S." means the United States Supreme Court; a court described by "Cir." is a federal appeals court, and federal courts whose abbreviated name includes "D." (for "District" Court) are federal trial courts. The "C.M.A." is the Court of Military Appeals. Dates of statutes refer to the year of publication, not the year of enactment. Citations are current to September 10, 1998.

Readers who wish to know more about the particular texts I have relied on, and the reasoning for some of the more intricate inferences I have drawn, may wish to consult my article "The Status/Conduct Distinction in the 1993 Revisions to Military Anti-Gay Policy: A Legal Archaeology," *GLQ* 3.2–3 (1996), on which this book is based. The article includes lengthy endnotes, omitted here, that explain many textual matters in excruciating detail. Many of the documents relied upon in this book appear at http://dont.stanford.edu, Stanford Law School's website on military anti-gay policy.

I. Government Documents

A. Statutes and Regulations

  1. Statutes

Family and Medical Leave Act of 1993, Pub.L. 103-03, § 601 (Sense of Congress statement).

10 U.S.C. § 654 (1993) (codifying National Defense Authorization Act for Fiscal Year 1994, Pub.L. 103-160 § 571, 107 Stat., 1547 (1994)) (the "Statute").

10 U.S.C. §§ 801–946 (1988) (Uniform Code of Military Justice, cited as "UCMJ").

Ga. Code Ann. § 16-6-2 (Michie 1984) (cited as "Georgia's sodomy statute").

  2. Federal Regulations

Exec. Order No. 9981, 3 C.F.R. § 722 (1943–1948) (Truman's order desegregating the armed services).

32 C.F.R. Ch. 1, Part 41 ("Enlisted Personnel Separations") (July 1, 1993 edition). Two different parts of "Appendix A: Separation Regulations," included in these regulations, are cited often. Appendix A is made up of Part 1 ("Reasons for Separation"), Part 2 ("Guidelines for Separation and Characterization"), and Part 3 ("Procedures for Separation"). Only a portion of Part 2 was revised in 1993 — subpart H, "Homosexuality." In this paper I have named Subpart H the "Old DOD Policy." It codifies DODD 1332.14 (Jan. 28, 1982) and DODD 1332.30 (Feb. 12, 1986). Everything else in Appendix A has remained in effect, and I have named it the "Separation Regulations." (DODD 1332.14 and DODD 1332.30 have been revised to guide enforcement of the Statute; see section I.A.3 of this bibliography, below.)

3. DOD Directives and Instructions

DODD1, DODD2, DODD3, DODI1 and DODI2 comprise the "Implementing Regulations." DODD means Department of Defense Directive; DODI means Department of Defense Instructions. (For Department of Defense documents that are not regulations, see section I.B.3 of this bibliography, below.)

DODD1: DODD 1304.26. "Qualification Standards for Enlistment, Appointment, and Induction" (Feb. 5, 1994).

Attachments to DODD1:

DODD1/a: DODD 1304.26, Enclosure 2. "Qualification Standards for Enlistment, Appointment, and Induction."

DODD1/b: DODD 1304.26, attachment. "Applicant Briefing Item on Separation Policy."

DODD1/c: DODD 1304.26, attachment. "Restrictions on Personal Conduct in the Armed Forces."

DODD2: DODD 1332.14. "Enlisted Administrative Separations" (Feb. 5, 1994).

Attachments to DODD2:

DODD2/a: DODD 1332.14, Enclosure 4-1. "Guidelines for Fact-Finding Inquiries into Homosexual Conduct."

DODD2/b: Amendments to DODD2/a (Feb. 28, 1994).

DODD3: DODD 1332.30. "Separation of Regular Commissioned Officers" (Feb. 5, 1994).

Attachments to DODD3:

DODD3/a: DODD 1332.14, Enclosure 4-1. "Guidelines for Fact-Finding Inquiries into Homosexual Conduct" (Feb. 5, 1994). (This document is identical to DODD2/a.)

DODD3/b: Amendments to DODD3/a (Feb. 28, 1994).

DODI1: DODI 5505.3. "Initiation of Investigations by Military Investigative Organizations" (July 11, 1986).

DODI2: DODI 5505.8. "Investigations of Sexual Misconduct by the Defense Criminal Investigative Organizations and Other DOD Law Enforcement Organizations" (Feb. 5, 1994).

Attachments to DODI2:

DODI2/a: "Investigations of Sexual Misconduct by Defense Criminal Investigative Organizations and Other DOD Law Enforcement Organizations."

DODI2/b: "Synopsis of Procedures for Criminal Investigations of Adult Private Consensual Sexual Misconduct."

4. Army Regulations

Army Reg. 635-200, Interim Change 102 (Headquarters, Department of the Army, Nov. 28, 1980).

Army Reg. 635-200, Change No. 39 (Nov. 23, 1972).

Army Reg. 635-100, Change No. 4 (Jan. 21, 1970).

Army Reg. 635-212, Change No. 8 (Jan. 21, 1970).

Army Reg. 135-178, Chap. 7-5b(6).

Army Reg. 635-89 (Oct. 1, 1968).

Army Reg. 635-89 (July 15, 1966).

Army Reg. 600-43 (April 10, 1953).

B. Executive and Legislative Branches

1. White House

WH1: "The President's News Conference" and "Memorandum on Ending Discrimination in the Armed Forces." *Weekly Comp. Pres. Doc.* 29 (Jan. 29, 1993): 108–12.

WH2: "White House Statement on Policy Regarding Homosexuals in the Miliary." *On Watch: Newsletter of the National Lawyers Guild Military Law Task Force* 15 (Mar. 1993): 2 (reprints the "Interim Policy").

WH3: "White House Background Briefing Concerning the Issue of Gays in the Military" (July 16, 1993) (Federal News Service transcript).

WH4: "Remarks Announcing the New Policy on Gays and Lesbians in the Military." *Weekly Comp. Pres. Doc.* 29 (July 19, 1993): 1369–73 (cited as the "Fort McNair speech").

2. Department of Justice

Reno, Janet. "Memorandum for the President: Defensibility of the New Policy on Homosexual Conduct in the Armed Forces" (July 19, 1993) (cited as the "Reno Memo").

3. Department of Defense

DOD1: "Department of Defense Regular Briefing" (May 10, 1993) (Federal News Service transcript).

DOD2: Office of the Secretary of Defense, "Summary Report of the Military Working Group" (July 1, 1993) (cited as the "Military Working Group Report" or "MWG Report").

DOD3: "Policy on Homosexual Conduct in the Armed Forces," memorandum from Secretary of Defense Les Aspin to the Secretaries of the Army, Navy, and Air Force and to the Chairman of the Joint Chiefs of Staff (July 19, 1993) (cited as the "New DOD Policy").

DOD4: "Policy Guidelines on Homosexual Conduct in the Armed Forces," attachment to New DOD Policy (cited as the "New DOD Policy Guidelines").

DOD5: "Remarks by the Joint Chiefs of Staff and Coast Guard Commandant Following Statement by President Clinton Announcing Policy on Gays in the Military Introduced by Secretary of Defense Les Aspin" (July 19, 1993) (Federal News Service transcript).

DOD6: "News Conference, Secretary of Defense Les Aspin, Jamie Gorelick, General Counsel, Department of Defense, Re: Regulations on Homosexual Conduct in the Military" (Dec. 22, 1993) (Federal News Service transcript).

DOD7: National Defense Research Institute. *Sexual Orientation and U.S. Military Personnel Policy: Options and Assessment, MR-323-OSD.* (RAND 1993) (cited as the "RAND Report").

DOD8: *DOD Policy on Homosexual Conduct Training Plan,* issued by Assistant Secretary of Defense Edwin Dorn, n.d., n.p.

DOD9: Memorandum of Judith A. Miller, General Counsel for the Department of Defense, for the General Counsels of the Miliary Departments, Re: Policy on Homosexual Conduct in the Armed Forces (Aug. 18, 1995).

4. Congress

Cong.1: Senate Hearings on the Family and Medical Leave Act of 1994, 139 *Cong. Rec.* S1262 (daily ed. Feb. 4, 1993) (cited as the "Mitchell Plan," adopted in the Act; see Statutes above).

Cong.2: "Policy Concerning Homosexuality in the Armed Forces."

Hearings before the Committee on Armed Services, U.S. Senate, 103d Congress, 2d Sess. (1993) (Mar. 29, 31; Apr. 29; May 7, 10, 11; July 20, 21, 22 hearings).

Cong.3: "News Conference on Opposition to 'Don't Ask, Don't Tell' Policy for Gays in the Military" (July 16, 1993) (Federal News Service transcript).

Cong.4: 139 *Cong. Rec.* S8876, 8877 (daily ed. July 16, 1993).

Cong.5: "Statement for Release by Senator Sam Nunn, Chairman, Senate Armed Services Committee" (July 19, 1993) (Federal News Service transcript).

Cong.6: "Capitol Hill Hearing with Defense Department Personnel: Hearing of the Senate Armed Services Committee" (July 20, 1993) (Federal News Service transcript).

Cong.7: Statement by Secretary of Defense Les Aspin before the House Committee on Armed Services (July 21, 1993) (cited as the "Aspin Statement").

C. Military Branches

1. Air Force

AF1: Department of the Air Force, Headquarters USAF/JAG, "Memorandum for All Staff Judge Advocates and Military Judges, Re: Commander Inquiries on Members Stating They Are Homosexual," (Nov. 3, 1993) (cited as the "Air Force JAG Memo").

AF2: Air Force JAG Memo, attachment 1, "Tips for Inquiry Officers of Cases Involving Members Who State They Are Homosexual."

AF3: Air Force JAG Memo, attachment 2, "Sample Questions for Inquiry Concerning Member Who States He Is Homosexual after Receiving Advanced Education Benefits."

2. Army

Army1: Commander's Inquiry, Sgt. Steven Spencer, pp. 1–2 (attachment to Able Complaint).

3. Marine Corps

MC1: U.S. Marine Corps Legal Service Support Section Policy Memorandum 2-93 Re: Detailing Counsel, Requests for Individual Military Counsel (IMC), Detailing Counsel for Respondent for Administrative Boards, and Providing Legal Advice by Defense Counsel (Aug. 24, 1993).

4. Navy

Navy1: Memorandum of Department of the Navy Code 34 Re: Homosexual Administrative Discharge Board/Show Cause Hearings (June 1994) (cited as the "Code 34 Memo").

D. Litigation and Other Advocacy

1. Decisional Law

Able

> *Able A: Able v. United States,* 847 F. Supp. 1038 (E.D.N.Y. 1994), *affirmed by* 44 F.3d 128 (2d Cir. 1995).
>
> *Able B: Able v. United States,* No. 94 CV 0974, 1995 WL 116322 (E.D.N.Y.) (Mar. 14, 1995).
>
> *Able C: Able v. United States,* 880 F. Supp. 968 (E.D.N.Y. 1995), *vacated and remanded by Able D.*
>
> *Able D: Able v. United States,* 88 F.3d 1280 (2d Cir. 1996), *vacating and remanding Able C.*
>
> *Able E: Able v. United States,* 968 F. Supp. 850 (1997).

Beller v. Middendorf, 632 F.2d 788 (9th Cir. 1980), *certiorari denied under the name Beller v. Lehman,* 452 U.S. 905, *and under the name Miller v. Weinberger,* 454 U.S. 855 (1981).

Ben-Shalom I (challenging discharge): *Ben-Shalom v. Secretary of the Army,* 489 F. Supp. 964 (E.D. Wis. 1980).

Ben-Shalom II (challenging refusal to reinstate)

> *Ben-Shalom II A: Ben-Shalom v. Marsh,* 703 F. Supp. 1372 (E.D. Wis.), *reversed by Ben-Shalom II B.*
>
> *Ben-Shalom II B: Ben-Shalom v. Marsh,* 881 F.2d 454 (7th Cir.), *reversing Ben-Shalom II A, certiorari denied under the name Ben-Shalom v. Stone,* 494 U.S. 1004 (1990).

Bowers v. Hardwick, 478 U.S. 186 (1986).

Cammermeyer v. Aspin, 850 F. Supp. 910 (W.D. Wa. 1994), *appeal dismissed as moot*, 97 F.3d 1235 (9th Cir. 1996).

Cleburne v. Cleburne Living Center, 473 U.S. 432 (1985).

Dahl v. Secretary of the United States Navy, 830 F. Supp. 1319 (E.D. Cal. 1993).

Dronenberg v. Zech, 741 F.2d 1388 (D.C. Cir. 1984).

Elzie v. Aspin, 841 F. Supp. 439 (D.D.C. 1993).

Equality Foundation

    Equality Foundation A: Equality Foundation of Greater Cincinnati v. City of Cincinnati, 860 F. Supp. 417 (S.D. Ohio 1994), *reversed by Equality Foundation B.*

    Equality Foundation B: Equality Foundation of Greater Cincinnati v. City of Cincinnati, 54 F.3d 261 (6th Cir. 1995), *reversing Equality Foundation A, vacated and remanded by* 116 S.Ct. 2519 (1996). **149**

    Equality Foundation C: Equality Foundation of Greater Cincinnati v. City of Cincinnati, 128 F.3d 289 (6th Cir. 1997), *petition for certiorari filed*, 66 U.S.L.W. 3749 (May 4, 1998).

Gay Law Students Association v. Pacific Telephone and Telegraph Company, 156 Cal. Rptr.14 (Cal. 1979).

Hatheway v. Secretary of the Army, 641 F.2d 1376 (9th Cir.), *certiorari denied by* 454 U.S. 864 (1981).

Heller v. Doe, 113 S.Ct. 2637 (1993).

High Tech Gays

    High Tech Gays A: High Tech Gays v. Defense Indus. Sec. Clearance Office, 668 F. Supp. 1361 (N.D. Cal. 1987), *reversed by High Tech Gays B.*

    High Tech Gays B: High Tech Gays v. Defense Indus. Sec. Clearance Office, 895 F.2d 563 (9th Cir. 1990), *reversing High Tech Gays A, and rehearing denied by High Tech Gays C.*

    High Tech Gays C: High Tech Gays v. Defense Indus. Sec. Clearance Office, 909 F.2d 375 (9th Cir.), *denying rehearing to High Tech Gays B.*

Holmes

    Holmes A: Holmes v. California Army National Guard, 920 F. Supp. 1510 (N.D. Cal. 1996), *reversed by Holmes B.*

Holmes B: *Holmes v. California Army National Guard*, 124 F.3d 1126 (9th Cir. 1997), *reversing Holmes A.*

Jantz v. Muci, 759 F. Supp. 1543 (D. Kan. 1991), *reversed by* 976 F.2d 623 (10th Cir. 1992), *certiorari denied by* 508 U.S. 952 (1993).

Matthews v. Marsh, 755 F.2d 182 (1st Cir. 1985).

Meinhold

Meinhold A: *Meinhold v. United States Department of Defense*, 62 Empl. Prac. Dec. ¶ 42,619 (C.D. Cal. Sept. 30, 1993), *stayed in part by Meinhold B.*

Meinhold B: *United States Department of Defense v. Meinhold*, 114 S.Ct. 374 (1993) (staying as much of the court's order in *Meinhold A* as granted relief to persons other than Meinhold).

Meinhold C: *Meinhold v. United States Department of Defense*, 34 F.3d 1469 (9th Cir. 1994), *affirming in part and reversing in part* 808 F. Supp. 1455 (C.D. Cal. 1993).

Padula v. Webster, 822 F.2d 97 (D.C. Cir. 1987).

Palmore v. Sidoti, 466 U.S. 429 (1984).

Philips

Philips A: *Philips v. Perry*, 883 F. Supp. 539 (W.D. Wash. 1995), *affirmed by Philips B.*

Philips B: *Philips v. Perry*, 106 F.3d 1420 (9th Cir. 1997).

Pruitt v. Cheney, 963 F.2d 1160 (9th Cir. 1991), *affirming in part and reversing in part* 659 F. Supp. 625 (C.D. Cal. 1987), *certiorari denied by* 113 S.Ct. 655 (1992).

Richenberg

Richenberg A: *Richenberg v. Perry*, 909 F. Supp. 1303 (D. Ne. 1995), *affirmed by Richenberg C.*

Richenberg B: *Richenberg v. Perry*, 73 F.3d 172 (8th Cir. 1995) (denying plaintiff's petition for an injunction pending appeal).

Richenberg C: *Richenberg v. Perry*, 97 F.3d 256 (4th Cir. 1996), *affirming Richenberg A, certiorari denied by* 118 S. Ct. 45 (1997).

Romer v. Evans, 517 U.S. 620 (1996).

Selland I (challenging separation under Old DOD Policy): *Selland v. Aspin*, 832 F. Supp. 12 (D.D.C. 1993) (granting preliminary injunction; suit later withdrawn by consent of the parties).

Selland II (challenging same separation under the Statute): 905 F. Supp. 260 (D. Md. 1995), *affirmed by* 100 F.3d 950 (4th Cir. 1996) (table),

certiorari denied under the name Selland v. Cohen by 117 S.Ct 1691
(1997).

Shahar v. Bowers, 114 F.3d 211 (11th Cir. 1997), *petition for hearing denied by* 120 F.3d 211 (11th Cir. 1997), *certiorari denied by* 118 S.Ct. 693 (1998).

Steffan

    Steffan A: Steffan v. Cheney, 733 F. Supp. 121 (D.D.C. 1989), *reversed by Steffan B.*

    Steffan B: Steffan v. Cheney, 920 F.2d 74 (D.C. Cir. 1990), *reversing Steffan A.*

    Steffan C: Steffan v. Cheney, 780 F. Supp. 1 (D.D.C. 1991), *reversed by Steffan D, in turn reversed by Steffan E.*

    Steffan D: Steffan v. Aspin, 8 F.3d 57 (D.C. Cir. 1993), *reversing Steffan C, and reversed by Steffan E.*

    Steffan E: Steffan v. Perry, 41 F.3d 677 (D.C. Cir. 1994) *(en banc), reversing Steffan D.*

151

Thomasson

    Thomasson A: Thomasson v. Perry, 895 F. Supp. 820 (E.D. Va. 1995), *affirmed by Thomasson B.*

    Thomasson B: Thomasson v. Perry, 80 F.3d 915 (4th Cir. 1996), *affirming Thomasson A, certiorari denied by* 117 S.Ct. 358 (1996).

Thorne

    Thorne A: Thorne v. United States Department of Defense, 916 F. Supp. 1358 (E.D. Va. 1996).

    Thorne B: Thorne v. United States Department of Defense, 945 F. Supp. 924 (1996), *affirmed by* 139 F.3d 893 (4th Cir. 1998), *petition for certiorari filed,* 67 U.S.L.W. 3038 (July 8, 1998).

United States v. Fagg, 34 M.J. 179 (C.M.A.), *certiorari denied by* 113 S.Ct. 92 (1992).

United States v. Henderson, 34 M.J. 174 (C.M.A. 1992).

United States Department of Agriculture v. Moreno, 413 U.S. 528 (1973).

Watkins

    Watkins A: Watkins v. United States Army, 551 F. Supp. 212 (W.D. Wash. 1982), *reversed by* 721 F.2d 687 (9th Cir. 1983).

    Watkins B: Watkins v. United States Army, 847 F.2d 1329 (9th Cir. 1988), *vacated by Watkins C.*

    Watkins C: Watkins v. United States Army, 875 F.2d 699 (9th Cir. 1989) (*en banc*), *vacating Watkins B, certiorari denied by* 498 U.S. 957 (1990).

Watson v. Perry, 918 F. Supp. 1403 (W.D. Wash. 1996), *affirmed by Holmes B.*

Williamson v. Lee Optical of Oklahoma, Inc., 348 U.S. 483 (1955).

Woodward v. United States, 871 F.2d 1068 (Fed. Cir. 1989), *certiorari denied by* 494 U.S. 1003 (1990).

2. Hearing Transcripts

Dunning Trans. Board of Inquiry in the Case of Lt. Maria Z. Dunning, SC, USNR-R. Conducted on November 29-30, and December 1, 1994.

Richenberg Trans. Board of Inquiry in the Case of Captain Richard F. Richenberg. Conducted on June 20–21, 1994.

3. Court Papers and Other Advocacy Documents

a. ABLE

CP1: Complaint for Declaratory Judgment and Injunctive Relief. In *Able v. United States.* 94 Civ. 0974 (E.D.N.Y) (Mar. 7, 1994).

CP2: Affidavit of David Braff. In *Able v. United States.* 94 Civ. 0974 (E.D.N.Y) (Mar. 4, 1994).

CP3: Plaintiffs' Trial Brief. In *Able v. United States.* 94 Civ. 0974 (E.D.N.Y.) (Mar. 7, 1995).

b. HARDWICK

CP4: Amicus Curiae Brief on Behalf of Respondents by Lambda Legal Defense and Education Fund, Inc. In *Bowers v. Hardwick.* No. 85-149 (U.S.) (Jan. 31, 1986).

c. Philips

CP5: Appellant's Opening Brief (Mark A. Philips). *Philips v. Perry.* No. 95-35293 (9th Cir.) (Aug. 14, 1995).

CP6: Reply Brief of Appellant (Mark A. Philips). *Philips v. Perry.* No. 95-35293 (9th Cir.) (Nov. 9, 1995).

d. Steffan

cp7: Defendants' Renewed Motion for Rule 37 Sanctions (Richard Cheney et al.). In *Steffan v. Cheney*. Civ. A. No. 88-3669 (D.D.C.) (Oct. 3, 1989).

cp8: Defendants' Reply Brief in Support of Its Renewed Motion for Rule 37 Sanctions (Richard Cheney et al.). In *Steffan v. Cheney*. Civ. A. No. 88-3669 (D.D.C.) (Oct. 24, 1989).

cp9: Brief for the Appellees (Richard Cheney, Secretary of Defense, et al.). In *Steffan v. Cheney*. No. 89-5476 (D.C. Cir.) (Sept. 19, 1990) (cited as the "Government's 1990 Brief").

cp10: Brief of Plaintiff-Appellant Joseph C. Steffan. In *Steffan v. Cheney*. No. 91-5409 (D.C. Cir.) (May 3, 1993).

cp11: Brief for Appellees (Secretary of Defense, et al.). In *Steffan v. Aspin*. No. 91-5409 (D.C. Cir.) (July 29, 1993) (cited as the "Government's 1993 Brief").

153

cp12: Brief for the Appellees (William D. Perry, Secretary of Defense, et al.). In *Steffan v. Perry*. No. 91-5409 (D.C. Cir.) (Mar. 28, 1994) (cited as the "Government's 1994 Brief").

e. Watson

Chapman Declaration: Declaration of Douglas G. Chapman and Plaintiff's Summary of Board Transcripts. In *Watson v. Perry*, No. 95-1141Z (W.D. Wash.) (Nov. 2, 1995).

Seven Exhibits 1 through 7. The Chapman Declaration summarizes and attaches seven exhibits produced by government lawyers in response to plaintiff Watson's request for documents "representing the records of the Board of Inquiry proceedings in 'statements' cases under [the Statute] in which the servicemembers have successfully rebutted the statutory presumption regarding homosexual acts or propensity" (Chapman Declaration 1–2). In every case the DOJ has made the transcripts anonymous by blacking out identifying personal and place names. The case files are cited in this paper by their exhibit number, as Seven Exhibits Nos. 1 through 7.

f. Advocacy to the Executive Branch

CP13: Memorandum of Michelle M. Benecke and C. Dixon Osburn to Judge Abner Mikva, Counsel to the President of the United States (May 31, 1995).

CP14: Letter of Jonathan M. Bowie to the Honorable Abner J. Mikva, Counsel to the President of the United States (Aug. 21, 1995).

II. Books, Articles, and Media

Agneshwar, Anand. "Powell on Sodomy: Ex-Justice Says He May Have Been Wrong." *National Law J.* (Nov. 5, 1990): 3.

Alexander, Janet Cooper. "Judges' Self-Interest and Procedural Rules: Comment on Macey." *J. Legal Stud.* 23 (1994): 647.

American Heritage Dictionary of the English Language. 2d ed. 1992.

Asad, Talal. "Ethnographic Representation, Statistics and Modern Power." *Social Research* 61 (1994): 55–88.

Austin, J. L. *How to Do Things with Words.* 2d ed. Cambridge, MA: Harvard UP, 1962.

Barnhart Dictionary of Etymology. Ed. Robert K. Barnhart. Bronx, NY: H. W. Wilson, 1988.

Barr, Stephen. "Hill Backs Gay Ban, Aspin Says; He Seeks Help of Joint Chiefs." *Washington Post* 25 Jan. 1993, final ed.: A1.

———. "Who's in Charge of the Military?" *New York Times* 26 Jan. 1993, late ed.: A22.

Benecke, Michelle M., and Kirstin S. Dodge. "Military Women in Nontraditional Fields: Casualties of the Armed Forces' War on Homosexuals." *Harvard Women's Law Journal* 13 (1990): 215–50.

Bérubé, Allan. *Coming Out under Fire: The History of Gay Men and Women in World War Two.* New York: Free, 1990.

Bérubé, Allan, and John D'Emilio. "The Military and Lesbians During the McCarthy Years." *Signs* 9 (1984): 759–75.

Blackstone, William. *Commentaries on the Laws of England.* Vol. 4 (1769). Rpt. Chicago: U of Chicago P, 1979.

Britton, Dana M., and Christine L. Williams. " 'Don't Ask, Don't Tell, Don't Pursue': Military Policy and the Construction of Heterosexual Masculinity." *Journal of Homosexuality* 3.1 (1995): 1–21.

Bronski, Michael. "Identity, Behavior, and the Military." *GLQ* 2 (1995): 307–17.

Bulmer, Martin, Kevin Bales, and Kathryn Kish Sklar, eds. *The Social Survey in Historical Perspective, 1880–1940.* New York: Cambridge UP, 1991.

Burr, Chandler. "Friendly Fire." *California Lawyer* June 1994: 54–100.

Butler, Judith. "Contagious Word: Paranoia and 'Homosexuality' in the Military." In *Excitable Speech: A Politics of the Performative.* New York: Routledge, 1997. 103–26.

Byrne, Edward M. *Military Law.* 3d ed. Annapolis, MD: Naval Institute P, 1981.

Carlson, Margaret. "Then There Was Nunn." *Time* 26 July 1993: 40–41.

Chauncey, George, Jr. "Christian Brotherhood or Sexual Perversion? Homosexual Identities and the Construction of Sexual Boundaries in the World War One Era." *Journal of Social History* 19 (1985): 189–211.

Clymer, Adam. "Lawmakers Revolt on Lifting the Ban in Military Service." *New York Times* 27 Jan. 1993, late ed.: A1.

Cole, David, and William N. Eskridge, Jr. "From Hand-Holding to Sodomy: First Amendment Protection of Homosexual (Expressive) Conduct." *Harvard Civil Rights-Civil Liberties Law Review* 29 (1994): 319–51.

Collins, Clinton, Jr. "Officer's Insubordination A Greater Threat than Gays in Uniform." *Star Tribune* 5 Feb. 1993, metro ed.: 19A.

Concise Oxford Dictionary of Current English. 1990 ed.

Crossfire. CNN. 19 July 1993. Interview with Robert Dornan. CNN transcript No. 879 (available in LEXIS, NEXIS library, CURNWS File).

Danziger, Kurt. "The Methodological Imperative in Psychology." *Philosophy of the Social Sciences* 15 (1985): 1–13.

———. "Statistical Method and the Historical Development of Research Practice in American Psychology." *Ideas in the Sciences.* Vol. 2 of *The Probabilistic Revolution.* Ed. Lorenz Krüger, Gerd Gigerenzer, and Mary S. Morgan. Cambridge, MA: MIT P, 1987. 36–47.

Devroy, Ann. "President Opens Military to Gays." *Washington Post* 20 July 1993, final ed.: A1.

Doe, Charles. "Aspin, Powell, Chiefs Defend Clinton Policy on Military Gays." 20 July 1993. United Press International, Washington News.

" 'Don't Ask, Don't Tell' Policy Embroils Marine." *Chicago Tribune* 12 Dec. 1994, north sports final ed.: 12.

Ewald, François. "Norms, Discipline, and the Law." *Law and the Order of Culture.* Ed. Robert Post. Berkeley: U of California P, 1991. 138–61.

Feeley, Malcolm, and Jonathan Simon. "Actuarial Justice: The Emerging New Criminal Law." *The Futures of Criminology.* Ed. David Nelkin. Thousand Oaks, CA: SAGE Publications, 1994. 173–201.

———. "The New Penology: Notes on the Emerging Strategy of Corrections and Its Implications." *Criminology* 30 (1992): 449–74.

Foucault, Michel. *The History of Sexuality.* Vol. 1. Trans. Robert Hurley. New York: Random House, 1980.

Friedman, Thomas L. "Accord is Reached on Military Rules for Gay Soldiers." *New York Times* 17 July 1993, late ed.: A1.

———. "Clinton Is Said to Accept Parts of Plan on Gay Ban." *New York Times* 16 July 1993, late ed.: A10.

———. "Legal Concerns Shaping New Military Gay Policy." *New York Times* 16 July 1993, natl. ed.: A7+.

"Gays in the Military: Clinton Meets Joint Chiefs Today." *The Hotline* 25 Jan. 1993: n.p.

Gilberd, Kathleen. "Crafting Equality: Elements of a Non-Discriminatory Policy." *On Watch: Newsletter of the National Lawyer's Guild Military Law Task Force* 25.4 (1993): 7–9.

Goldberg, Jonathan, ed. *Reclaiming Sodom.* New York: Routledge, 1994.

———. *Sodometries: Renaissance Texts, Modern Sexualities.* Stanford: Stanford UP, 1992.

Hacking, Ian. "How Should We Do the History of Statistics?" *I & C* 8 (1981): 15–26.

———. "Making Up People." *Reconstructing Individualism: Autonomy, Individuality, and the Self in Western Thought.* Ed. Thomas C. Heller, Morton Sosna, and David E. Wellbery. Stanford: Stanford UP, 1986. 222–36.

———. *The Taming of Chance.* Cambridge: Cambridge UP, 1990.

Halley, Janet E. "The Politics of the Closet: Toward Equal Protection for Gay, Lesbian and Bisexual Identity." *UCLA Law Review* 36 (1989): 915–76.

———. "Reasoning about Sodomy: Act and Identity in and after *Bowers v. Hardwick*." *Virginia Law Review* 79 (1993): 1721–80.

Halperin, David M. "More or Less Gay-Specific." Rev. of *Homos*, by Leo Bersani. *London Review of Books* 23 May 1996: 24–27.

Healy, Melissa. "Clinton Aides Urge Quick End to Military Ban on Gays." *Los Angeles Times* 8 Jan. 1993, home ed.: A1.

Howlett, Debbie. "Aviator Is First Gay Put on Inactive Reserve." *USA Today* 7 May 1993, final ed.: 2A.

Hunter, Nan D. "Life after *Hardwick*." *Harvard Civil Rights-Civil Liberties Law Review* 27 (1992): 531–54.

James, Fleming, Jr., Geoffrey C. Hazard, Jr., and John Leubsdorf. *Civil Procedure*. 4th ed. Boston: Little, Brown, 1992.

Karst, Kenneth L. "The Pursuit of Manhood and the Desegregation of the Armed Forces." *UCLA Law Review* 38 (1991): 499–581.

Kavanagh, Kay. "Don't Ask, Don't Tell: Deception Required, Disclosure Denied." *Psychology, Public Policy, and Law* 1 (1995): 142–60.

Lancaster, John. "Joint Chiefs Take Hypothetical Test on Gay Policy." *Washington Post* 22 July 1993, final ed.: A4.

———. "Senators Find Clinton Policy on Gays in Military Confusing." *Washington Post* 21 July 1993, final ed.: A12.

Lippman, Thomas W. "Pentagon Studies Conflict on Effect of Gays in the Military." *Washington Post* 27 Aug. 1993, final ed.: A10.

Lochead, Carolyn. "Senate Panel Votes to Tighten Gay Directive: Nunn Says Measure Clarifies Clinton's Military Policy." *San Francisco Chronicle* 24 July 1993, final ed.: A4.

Mazur, Diane. "The Unknown Soldier: A Critique of 'Gays in the Military' Scholarship and Litigation." *U.C. Davis Law Review* 29 (1996): 223–81.

Miles, Sara. "Don't Ask, It's Hell." *Out* February 1995: 61–65, 108–10.

"Military Budget Is Passed; Includes New Gay Policy." *New York Times* 18 Nov. 1993, natl. ed.: A8.

Morganthau, Tom. "Gays and the Military." *Newsweek* 1 Feb. 1993: 52–55.

Murdoch, Joyce. "Sailor Who Disclosed Homosexuality Now Finds Himself in Legal Limbo; At Least 100 in Military Are Affected by Clinton Compromise." *Washington Post* 8 Feb. 1993, final ed.: A6.

Murphy, Lawrence R. *Perverts by Official Order: The Campaign against Homosexuals by the United States Navy.* New York: Harrington, 1988.

Oxford English Dictionary. 2d ed. 1989.

Raddatz, Martha. "Marine Might Be Discharged for Thinking He Might Be Gay." *Morning Edition.* National Public Radio, 8 June 1994 (retrieved from, and available on, LEXIS).

"A Retreat on Gay Soldiers." *New York Times* 19 Sept. 1993, late ed.: A16.

Schmalz, Jeffrey. "Difficult First Step." *New York Times* 15 Nov. 1992, late ed., sec. 1: 22.

———. "Gay Groups Regrouping for War on Military Ban." *New York Times* 7 Feb. 1993, late ed.: A26.

Schmitt, Eric. "A Compromise on Military's Gay Ban is Discussed." *New York Times* 23 June 1993, late ed.: A20.

———. "In Break for Clinton, Nunn Lends Support to Gay-Troop Ban." *New York Times* 21 July 1993, late ed.: A1.

———. "Joints [*sic*] Chiefs Hear Clinton Again Vow to Ease Gay Policy." *New York Times* 26 Jan. 1993, late ed.: A1.

———. "Military Praises Gay Policy for Ambiguity and Caution." *New York Times* 22 July 1993, late ed.: A14.

———. n.t. *New York Times* 8 July 1993, late ed.: A16.

———. "Pentagon Chief Warns Clinton on Gay Policy." *New York Times* 25 Jan. 1993, late ed.: A1.

———. "Pentagon Keeps Silent on Rejected Gay Troop Plan." *New York Times* 23 July 1993, late ed.: A12.

———. "Pentagon Speeds Plan to Lift Gay Ban." *New York Times* 16 Apr. 1993, late ed.: A20.

———. "White House and Chiefs Snagged on Retaining Gay-Ban Language." *New York Times* 2 July 1993, late ed.: A1.

Shilts, Randy. *Conduct Unbecoming: Lesbians and Gays in the U.S. Military, Vietnam to the Persian Gulf.* New York: St. Martin's, 1993.

Simon, Jonathan. "The Ideological Effects of Actuarial Practices." *Law & Society Review* 22 (1988): 771–800.

Talk of the Nation, Federal Document Clearing House (Jan. 1, 1998) (available on WESTLAW at 1998WL2933498).

Terkel, Studs. *"The Good War": An Oral History of World War Two.* New York: Pantheon, 1984.

Thomas, Kendall. "Beyond the Privacy Principle." *Columbia Law Review* 92 (1992): 1431–516.

———. "Shower/Closet." *Assemblage* 20 (1993): 80–81.

Valdes, Francisco. "Sexual Minorities in the Military: Charting the Constitutional Frontiers of Status and Conduct." *Creighton Law Review* 27 (1994): 384–475.

Warner, Michael. Introduction to *Fear of a Queer Planet: Queer Politics and Social Theory.* Ed. Warner. Minneapolis: U of Minnesota P, 1993. vii–xxxi.

Webster's Ninth New Collegiate Dictionary. 1987 ed.

West, Louis Joylon, William T. Doidge, and Robert L. Williams. "An Approach to the Problem of Homosexuality in the Military Service." *American Journal of Psychiatry* 115.5 (1958): 392–401.

Library of Congress Cataloging-in-Publication Data
Halley, Janet E.
Don't : a reader's guide to the military's anti-gay
policy / Janet E. Halley.
p.   cm. — (Public planet books)
Includes bibliographical references.
ISBN 0-8223-2285-4 (cloth : alk. paper).
ISBN 0-8223-2317-6 (pbk. : alk. paper)
1. United States—Armed Forces—Gays—Government policy.
2. Gays—Legal status, laws, etc.—United States.
3. United States—Military policy.   4. Discrimination—United States.
I. Title.   II. Series.
UB418.G38H35   1999   355'.0086'6420973—dc21   98-38580   CIP